THE WALKING DEAD

MAGAZINE COMPANION

TITAN

WWW.TITAN-COMICS.COM

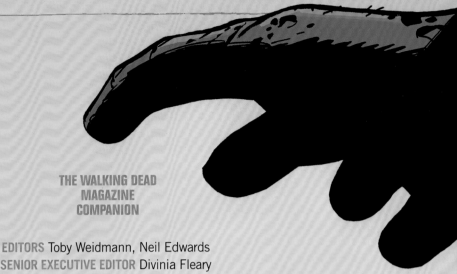

THE WALKING DEAD MAGAZINE COMPANION

EDITORS Toby Weidmann, Neil Edwards
SENIOR EXECUTIVE EDITOR Divinia Fleary
DESIGNER Russell Seal
SENIOR PRODUCTION CONTROLLER Jackie Flook
PRODUCTION CONTROLLER Peter James
ART DIRECTOR Oz Browne
SENIOR SALES MANAGER Steve Tothill
PRESS OFFICER Will O'Mullane
DIRECT SALES/MARKETING MANAGER Ricky Claydon
PUBLISHING MANAGER Darryl Tothill
PUBLISHING DIRECTOR Chris Teather
OPERATIONS DIRECTOR Leigh Baulch
EXECUTIVE DIRECTOR Vivian Cheung
PUBLISHER Nick Landau

Acknowledgements...
Titan would like to thank everyone at Skybound for their help in
putting this volume together.

ISBN: 9781785862984

Published by Titan,
a division of Titan Publishing Group, Ltd.
144 Southwark Street,
London SE1 0UP.
The Walking Dead is TM and © 2017,
Robert Kirkman, LLC.

Collecting material previously
published in The Walking Dead Magazine.

First edition, December 2017

10 9 8 7 6 5 4 3 2 1

Printed in China.

THE WALKING DEAD

MAGAZINE COMPANION

CONTENTS

In our last book, Robert Kirkman talked about how he goes about creating and writing characters in *The Walking Dead* comic. This time around it's regular series artist Charlie Adlard's turn to reveal his creative processes for new and established characters. Over the next few pages, Adlard explains how he takes Kirkman's written descriptions and translates them into the visual representations we all know and love. INTERVIEW: Nick Jones

British artist Charlie Adlard has been the regular illustrator on *The Walking Dead* since issue seven, also taking over cover art duties from issue 25. Despite a geographical distance between Adlard and Robert Kirkman – the former is based in the heart of the UK, the latter in the US – the working relationship between artist and writer could not be closer, and they must surely be recognized as one of the foremost creative partnerships working in comic books today.

As Kirkman previously explained to *TWDM*, the creation of *The Walking Dead*'s characters, both old and new, is very much a collaborative process between the two. Sometimes Kirkman has a very clear picture for a character, which Adlard must then translate into an illustration, but more often than not, the writer trusts the artist to use his own imagination to inform the look of the people who inhabit the world of the dead. Twelve years in and 150-odd issues later, it's clear that this system not only works, but has also played a key role in *The Walking Dead*'s ongoing success.

Here's what Adlard had to say about the creative process…

Is creating characters an easy process for you?
It's fairly easy. The trick with *The Walking Dead* is not trying to create outlandish characters. You want to ground everything in a certain reality, because the comic is based in reality – apart from the fact it's the zombie apocalypse. So the trick is to create recognizable characters that don't have costumes, don't have peculiar hair and so on… I try to create interesting people using the template of ordinariness.

Take us through the process of creating a new character.
I'm embarrassed to say about 90 per cent of the characters are created on the page. Certain characters have become prominent more by default than pre-destiny, and those are the frustrating ones, because they suddenly pop to the fore and you think, 'I wish I'd spent a bit more time on creating that one.' Certain characters – like Ezekiel, Michonne, the Governor, Negan

> ## "I TRY TO CREATE INTERESTING PEOPLE USING THE TEMPLATE OF ORDINARINESS."

– had a bit more work on them since they are, arguably, of a small band that are 'outrageous.'

Does Robert Kirkman warn you in advance that these will be important characters?
Yes. With those four that I just mentioned, Robert would have said something along the lines of, "He/she is going to be in this book as a major player."

But even if he doesn't mention it, sometimes you get the impression… When Ezekiel popped

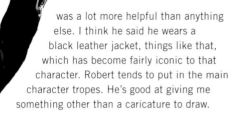

up, I just thought, 'Well, he's the leader of this community, therefore he's going to be in this book for a considerable time.' Then I spend a bit longer, do a few character sketches, go backwards and forwards – but it's never much.

"ONE OF THE MOST HELPFUL THINGS ANY WRITER CAN DO IS DESCRIBE A CHARACTER LOOKING LIKE A FAMOUS PERSON."

We understand that Robert will often send you a sketch if he has something specific in mind.
Well, Robert's sketches leave a lot to be desired! [*Laughs*] No, he's quite helpful. Actually, one of the most helpful things any writer can do, not just Robert, is to describe the character looking like a famous person, whether it's a TV star, a pop star or whatever. It gives you that instant, 'Ah, I've got the face now.' Then you can run with that look and do your version of them.

I'm sure every writer has an idea of what their character looks like in their head derived from something they've seen, whether it's from TV, film, friends, relatives, and so on. Just saying something like that can be a lot more helpful than lines and lines of dialogue and description.

So you prefer as little description as possible?
There are certain essentials... I can't remember, for instance, exactly how we designed Negan, but I remember Robert saying something like he's thickset... I don't think he even said he's got short black hair, but he did describe him as a certain personality, which

"I'VE NEVER STRUGGLED WITH THE MORE OUTLANDISH CHARACTERS. THEY ARE THE EASIER AND MORE FUN ONES TO DRAW."

was a lot more helpful than anything else. I think he said he wears a black leather jacket, things like that, which has become fairly iconic to that character. Robert tends to put in the main character tropes. He's good at giving me something other than a caricature to draw.

Are there any characters you have struggled to get right?
Plenty! Funnily enough, I've never struggled with the more outlandish characters. The easier and more fun ones to draw are the Governor, Michonne, and Ezekiel. Because they have such distinctive looks, you're not so concerned about getting the facial aspects right; you know people

are going to recognize them instantly, and they tend to wear roughly the same clothes.

However, I'm very aware of not giving the characters costumes. I don't like to see Michonne constantly wearing exactly the same gear that she might have worn a week ago, because you wouldn't do that in real life. Even more so now we've done the two-year leap, where the characters aren't out in the wilderness all the time and have more than one set of clothes.

It sounds a bit controversial, but I was quite glad when we killed Glenn, because I always struggled with him. The problem was when he and Maggie went to get their hair cut in the prison,

9

I was drawing them and thinking, 'Christ, they look exactly the same now!' Especially as they were [both] in prison clothes as well. The only advantage we had was Glenn tended to wear a baseball cap, but again, I was aware that in reality he wouldn't constantly have worn it. So when he died, I thought, 'At least I've only gotta draw one of them now!'

When there isn't a character description, how do you go about creating them?
They pretty much come from my imagination. A good example is this script I'm working on at the moment, for issue 153; there's a character that's in it for a few pages and Robert's noted, "His name's this. Just choose a character that you've casually drawn in a crowd scene." If you've got a crowd scene, you're just randomly thinking up faces and looks. So what I will do for that character – if he becomes a major character it will be the bane of my life – I'll go back and look at the last crowd scene I drew and pick a face from there.

I've got a couple of really good reference books I've picked up over the years – photography books of people, which are just faces, quite unique faces as well, and that gives me a load of inspiration if I'm really struggling. And, I've got good ol' Google image search, which is pretty much your essential tool nowadays.

How observant do you think you have to be as an artist?
Oh, very observant. I'm constantly looking and just clocking things in my mind... Whether it stays in my mind is something else. But if I'm sat in town in a coffee shop, I will people-watch and try to remember faces, movements and so on. I think most artists do that. But I don't sit there and sketch people – I always get a bit self-conscious about that; people think you're a bit weird.

> "IF I'M SAT IN A COFFEE SHOP, I PEOPLE-WATCH AND TRY TO REMEMBER FACES, MOVEMENTS AND SO ON. I THINK MOST ARTISTS DO THAT."

The comic has been running so long now, characters change and grow old. Are there tricks you use to keep a character recognizable?
I didn't really do anything up until the time-jump, because roughly the period covered before that jump was a year and half, two years, so the adults won't change much. Without access to razor blades and things like that, they might grow beards – I was conscious of that, hair growing and so on.

But I was most conscious about the children. Carl I was trying to portray slightly older as the comic went on. It's tricky; as we all know, kids, especially at Carl's age – he starts off about seven or eight – are gonna change considerably. I've got a

10 and 14-year-old – I know! And the younger they are, the more radical the change is.

After the jump, with the adults, even in two years they're not gonna change much – the look might change, as we portrayed – but the kids again were the ones that would radically change. Carl, by that time, had adult proportions. He had a young face, but now was 13 or 14 – so

that's getting to be adult size. That was probably the most significant change that I had to do to any of the characters in the whole of *The Walking Dead*. I've always said, children are the hardest to draw, because you add one little line and you've aged them two or three years. The trick is almost to take out stuff more than add it.

"CHILDREN ARE HARD TO DRAW, BECAUSE YOU ADD ONE LITTLE LINE AND YOU'VE AGED THEM TWO OR THREE YEARS."

With so many characters portrayed over 150 issues, do you have anything you use as reference to keep them all individual and make sure you know who everyone is?
It's just a case of referring back to previous issues. I have a table by my drawing board with all the trades piled up. I do tend to refer back to earlier drawings of the characters, just so I can hopefully find a consistent through-line rather than just a previous issue. But someone like Rick, the big main characters, I hardly refer back to anymore because I've drawn them for so long it's almost second nature now.

The characters we haven't really spoken about are the walkers, who have been decaying for several years now. How do you address that?
That's a bit of a challenge. I'm very conscious of the fact that the majority of the walkers are slowly decaying. I mean there'll always be new ones as well, but I'm very aware that there are less new ones. It's hard to do that day-to-day, but over a time period I like to think that there seem to be more bald zombies nowadays, more really emaciated zombies, than there were perhaps 10 years ago.

What do you use for inspiration for the walkers?
I just make them up as I go along. Of this great

OPPOSITE PAGE, TOP: This will be hard for Glenn fans to hear, but Adlard was happy when the character was killed because he was the character he most struggled to draw. THIS PAGE, ABOVE & TOP: Children change so much in their formative years it can be hard to ensure they still look like their younger selves. LEFT: The walkers have been steadily decaying over the series' run – and the hair is the first thing to go! BELOW: Adlard never needs to remind himself of what the main characters look like, such as Rick. But then he has been drawing them for a very long time.

reality-based franchise that we are in control of, *that* is the pure fantasy element and one you can have fun with. I'm not nipping down the local morgue every other weekend to get my inspiration. [*Laughs*] I've rarely looked at wounds or anything like that; zombies are the fun element.

The beauty of zombies is you can draw them slightly badly and just say, "Ah, yeah, it's because he's broken his arm in a slightly weird place." You can get away with *a lot* with zombies!

Are there any attributes you feel a comic book artist needs?
The ability to tell a story is essential. I know that sounds really obvious, but at conventions people come up to me and show me their work, and so many just have single images. I just think, 'Why are you showing me single images, if you want to draw comics?' The first thing you need to do is show that you can tell a story. You might be the best artist in the world, you might be the Vincent van Gogh of comic books, but you're not gonna get very far if your storytelling is rubbish. •

EVERYTHING YOU NEED TO KNOW ABOUT THE WALKERS

IT'S THROUGH DESIGN THAT WE KNOW VERY LITTLE ABOUT THE UNDEAD: WE DON'T KNOW WHAT CAUSED THE OUTBREAK; WE DON'T KNOW WHAT CAUSES THE DEAD TO RISE AGAIN; AND WE DON'T REALLY KNOW WHAT DRIVES THEM TO DESIRE RAW FLESH. BUT THROUGHOUT *THE WALKING DEAD*'S RUN WE HAVE GLEANED CERTAIN THINGS ABOUT THEM. OVER THE NEXT FEW PAGES, *TWDM* COLLATES EVERYTHING WE HAVE LEARNT ABOUT THE UNDEAD FROM THE PAGES OF THE COMIC THROUGH TO THE ACTION ON OUR TV SCREENS. WORDS: DAN AUTY

fter 10 years and more than 150 issues of the comic, six seasons of the AMC TV show, a companion series now in its third year, and any number of video and board games, it is easy to take zombies for granted. While their presence in the world of *The Walking Dead* ultimately informs every decision that the characters make, they are now an accepted part of the world. For the most part, the heroes of the series know how to deal with them, and the threat they pose is far less than that of other humans. But the zombies are still there, and the long-term survival of humanity relies on understanding exactly how they behave and what can be done to stop them.

The Walking Dead originator, Robert Kirkman, has made no secret

of the massive influence that George Romero's zombie movies have had on his work, and his walkers more or less follow the 'rules' laid down by Romero in 1968's *Night Of The Living Dead*. But even Romero didn't stick hard-and-fast to these throughout his films, and naturally, there have been a vast number of other zombie films, TV shows and stories released in the decades since. How do *The Walking Dead*'s zombies stand apart? What do we actually know about them?

IN THE BEGINNING

In both the comic and the show, our introduction to the zombie outbreak is the same. Rick wakes from a coma in hospital, to find a world quickly becoming overrun by the living dead. No warning,

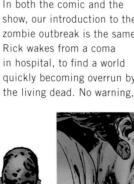

no build-up – we were thrown straight in, with our hero fighting for his life against this new, unknown enemy. The first few issues and episodes quickly established the rules and principal behavior of the undead, but was there any warning that could have been heeded?

The big problem is communication between those surviving, as the outbreak took control so quickly, that it's hard to piece together any coherent narrative. Everyone's story is different and yet the same – friends and families are attacked, die and return. Even the companion show, AMC's *Fear The Walking Dead*, set at the start of the outbreak, provides few clues about its origins – again, the focus is on the survival of the characters, not how the situation started.

As Kirkman himself has said: "It is not the priority in *The Walking Dead*. Every other story deals with that stuff and we're concerned about the heart."

PASS IT ON

So, if we don't know how it started, what do we know about the physiology of the pathogen that causes reanimation? A key episode occurs in season one of the show, and provides one of the only times – in any medium – that an actual scientist speaks about the outbreak. The final episode of

WE STILL DON'T KNOW... ...How the outbreak started. And it's quite possible that we will never know, as Robert Kirkman has stated he's more interested in telling stories about the 'now,' rather than the 'then.' He's teased illumination in the past – most memorably through Eugene Porter, who fooled us all into thinking he had a potential cure for the virus – but there's been nothing concrete to explain the outbreak. Doesn't stop fans from speculating though.

show and the comic, from the very start. And despite Dale's morbid hilarity that the Hunter cannibals are eating "tainted meat" after they tuck into his leg (replaced by Bob Stookey in season five of the show), unknowing that he had recently been bitten, they do not seem to suffer any particularly negative reaction to digesting it.

There is also a difference between the way the TV show and comic deals with walker blood entering the human bloodstream. In issue 122 of the comic, Negan prepares for an attack on the Hilltop by coating his spiked bat, Lucille, in zombie goo, before instructing his men to do the same with their weapons. "We're going to have space-aged zombie bacteria weapons at our disposal!" he declares. And it works – every Hilltop resident hit with one of the Saviors' arrows or blades succumbs to infection and dies in the following days.

On the show, however, this is simply not the case. In season two, Shane cuts himself with a knife previously used to kill a walker, and much later, the same thing happens when Sasha accidentally cuts Abraham with a blade covered in walker blood. In both cases, the recipient of the wound remains alive and well.

SENSE AND SENSIBILITY

While zombies are slow and mindless, they know how to do one thing – find humans to eat. People spend much of *The Walking Dead* keeping a low profile, so that walkers remain unaware of their presence. But how exactly do zombies become aware that a tasty snack is close-by?

that season introduces the character of Dr Edwin Jenner, a disease control expert who tells Rick in private that everyone in the world is carrying the virus. It doesn't matter how you die, you *will* return as a zombie once it happens – hence the zombification of Shane and Randall, neither of whom were killed by walkers. It is actually the return of Shane that prompts Rick to share Jenner's information with the rest of the group.

The rapid death that occurs following a walker bite is, therefore, due to infection, and there is a suggestion that the virus reduces the immune system generally, given how quickly a walker bite can kill, no matter how small. In addition, many of the survivors in the prison in season four became dangerously ill when faced with flu-like symptoms, their immune systems completely breaking down.

However, while a bite kills, close contact with walker flesh and fluid does not necessarily. The trick of smearing zombie gore on the body to disguise the smell of a human has been used on numerous occasions in both the

...What happens to the food they eat. We've seen walkers devour humans, horses, tigers, deer and so on, but how is this meat processed by their bodies? OK, it's not the most pleasant of subjects, but living people eventually have to excrete the food and liquids they consume. We're not sure walkers are too bothered about finding a washroom, but that food waste has to go somewhere, right? If they don't go to the toilet, surely there would be a lot more extremely bloated walkers out there, with bellyfuls of undigested meat.

It's clear that as well as reanimating motor functions, the virus also allows the return of some senses. But although it would initially seem that walkers can smell their intended prey – hence the aforementioned decisions to disguise human aroma with zombie viscera – we can deduce that what they can actually smell is other walkers. There are plenty of occasions where walkers have staggered right past concealed humans without detecting their aroma. The scenes where zombie gunk is used as body paint – seen most recently in season's six's escape from the Alexandria horde – is to give a survivor the same stench as everyone else. Not smelling like a corpse is the giveaway; if a walker sees you and you don't smell bad, he's coming for you. As Andrea says in season one: "They smell dead, we don't. It's pretty distinct."

A walker is also able to hear

– the reason Rick and his group use blades (or in Daryl's case, crossbow bolts) rather than guns is as much to stop attracting other walkers as it is to conserve bullets. Whether these senses are deteriorating over time is unclear, but Kirkman's suggestion in interviews, that the body's decay continues even after zombification, would suggest that they are.

MOB TACTICS

Understanding how walkers behave, both individually and in groups, has been crucial to surviving in this dangerous world. There are many examples of the undead moving in packs, often termed a herd, in a specific direction. Usually this is towards a common goal – lunch or a sound – but there is also a suggestion that a walker will imitate the behavior of other zombies. In issue 60, Eugene explains: "If one of them even so much as brushes a hand against your door – and another one sees that, mistakes it as an attempt to get in – it's over. That one starts trying to get in – the one who did the accidental tap thinks something's inside all of a sudden – he starts beating on the door with him."

It is also noticeable how a walker's behavior becomes more aggressive when moving en-masse. The fact that a huge cluster of walkers can become a mass of snarling jaws and clawing limbs implies that some vestige of emotion remains. What we would call a 'mob mentality' in humans still plays a part in the psychological make-up of a zombie.

PLAYING DEAD

While the majority of walkers do just that – walk – there are those that stay where they are, waiting for their prey to come to them. These are usually referred to as 'lurkers' – this term occurs predominantly in the comic book and video games, although the behavior can be seen in all formats.

In the comic book, Allen is killed by a lurker in the prison, while on the show Hershel is bitten by a zombie seemingly 'playing dead.' The tactic implies a shred of instinct, as if the desire for food has led even the most primitive, intelligence-starved zombie brain to develop an alternative method to find lunch.

…What's really happening outside of the US. It would make sense that the contagion is a worldwide pandemic and we did learn that Spain at least has also been overrun, as seen in one-shot 'The Alien,' written by Brian K Vaughan and sanctioned as canon by Robert Kirkman. Claudia says she's trying to get to the US because, "Word on the street is that your government has found a way to contain the outbreak." Could this be true, or is it just a lot of hooey spread by rumor?

GRAVE RAMIFICATIONS

So if dying, whether from a walker bite or other causes, has the same result, how long can we expect a corpse to stay lying down? It seems to vary – sometimes reanimation seems almost instantaneous, such as Shane on the TV show, and sometimes a victim will lie in a fever for hours before returning, as with Morgan in the comic. When Rick met Dr Jenner, he is told: "We had reports of it happening in as little as three minutes. The longest we heard of was eight hours."

PLEASED TO MEAT YOU

As for the walker's desire for human flesh, one can perhaps surmise that the need to eat is so primal, that it remains a singular driving force after reanimation. And it doesn't have to be human flesh.

As early as the second episode of the original show, a horse provides a tasty snack for a horde of walkers, while episode three of *Fear The Walking Dead* features the zombie consumption of a dog

in a key scene. The latter scene (the episode is actually called 'The Dog') illustrates why there are so few domesticated animals around in the main show. Animals that had been living so close to humans for so long had no reason to expect that their owners were about to start eating them when the outbreak started.

Whether a zombie eats man or beast, we know that the meat gets as far as their stomachs. In season two, Rick and Daryl cut into a walker's belly to see if it had consumed Sophia, and after Lori is eaten in season three we see the walker in question sitting around with a distended belly full of, er, Lori, thankfully sans baby. What happens beyond that is unclear – if the full digestion system works, and it comes out the other end, there is little evidence of it. More likely, a walker will simply burst if their body cannot hold any more food.

The comic and the TV show do differ slightly when it comes to the importance of food to a walker. In the latter, there is never any suggestion that a zombie needs to eat, it is just part of their basic drive. The

HUUUNNNHH.

LOOK AT HIM--LOOK AT HOW HE'S NOT MOVING AT ALL. I'M RIGHT HERE--HE CAN BARELY OPEN HIS MOUTH TO BITE ME.

THIS IS FASCINATING.

IT'S LIKE HE KNOWS HE SHOULD--HE WANTS TO BITE ME--BUT HE'S TOO WEAK.

comic, however, does introduce the concept that a prolonged period without food causes increased weakness. In issue 55, after witnessing a lurker that can barely raise himself from the ground, Eugene theorizes that it might in fact be malnourished.

COLD SWEAT

So, if a zombie can survive without food, what about survival in other circumstances? Does climate make a difference? The warm southern weather of much of the show and the comic is clearly conducive to a walker's existence, but there are also a few examples of how they cope in other environments. We've seen that cold does have an effect on them, and they can freeze; but they also thaw out and carry on as before. A frozen walker is encountered in the snowbound pages of issue eight, unable to move but still making vague sounds.

WE STILL DONT KNOW...

...If there's a cure. So we kind of know that the zombie infection is some kind of very aggressive virus that resides in all living humans (animals seem unaffected), which is activated upon death. Could there be a cure for this? Potentially. It's probably too late for the ones who have already turned – after all, they are already dead, so a cure would just turn them back into carcasses – but for the living, their outlook is pretty bleak without one.

As Rick says: "I guess they don't have blood pumping through them… they must freeze faster than us." And the decision to stay in the Wiltshire Estates has dire consequences in the following issue, when the ice starts to melt on the ground and the frozen undead inhabitants thaw out.

As for water, a zombie certainly can't swim, but since it doesn't breathe either, it can't drown. In season four, the Governor stabs Pete then dumps his weighted body in a lake. That episode ends with a zombie Pete submerged in the water, hungrily reaching for his murderer, who stands above him on dry land, looking down.

In addition, prolonged exposure to water makes a walker bloat in a particularly disgusting way. Witness the gloopy zombie trapped down the well on Hershel's farm, or the cellar full of grotesque, slimy walkers in the flooded basement of a foodbank in season five.

OVER AND OUT

If there's one thing that is vital for every survivor it is how to kill a walker. There's only one way: a decisive brain injury. A bullet does the trick, but so does a blade or hard impact, and any part of the head seems vunerable. As Dr Jenner reveals in season one, brain reactivation is simultaneous with the body's reanimation, we can surmise that the former causes the latter.

As a result, brain trauma removes the ability for the body to function. A severed body part cannot move on its own – however, a severed head will maintain its muscular functions, as long as the brain remains intact. And if the zombies are indeed continuing to rot, then their brains will eventually decay past the point of continued activity. Sadly, it seems unlikely that the remaining human population will be around to see a point when every walker brain has rotted. It's a walker's world.

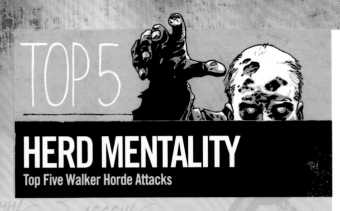

TOP 5

HERD MENTALITY
Top Five Walker Horde Attacks

5. SURROUNDED!
The first time the word 'herd' is used is by Eugene in issue 53 and, while Rick and the others have faced packs of zombies before, their first true experience of a herd/horde comes six issues later. The run-in happens after a bunch of the gang pick up Morgan and stop by the police station in search of weapons. A massive group of the ugly undead surround Rick, Morgan, Carl, and Abraham in their car and, with nowhere near the manpower required to fight, they are left with no choice but to run. ◇◇◇◇◇◇◇◇◇◇◇◇◇◇◇◇◇◇◇◇◇◇◇◇◇◇◇◇

4. BETTER THE DEVIL YOU KNOW...
There's something particularly interesting about the way our heroes respond to the swarm of walkers that surges through the fences at the prison: for starters, their presence is barely even acknowledged. The group is far more concerned about the threat posed by the human invasion taking place, as the Governor and his Woodbury army rain bullets down on them. In many ways, it's a pivotal moment that blurs the lines between the symbolic darkness of the undead and the malevolent nature of humanity, in its darkest of days. ◇◇◇◇◇◇◇◇◇

3. OH, CRAP!
Following the death of Douglas Monroe's wife, Rick and the gang are finally given the opportunity to step up and lead Alexandria. It's damn good timing, too, because in issue 79 the group finds the walls of the community surrounded by walkers – a result of too much gunplay. Tut-tut! Now, let's be honest here, it's not like the native Alexandrians could have dealt with the problem. It takes a certain 'skill.' The image of the hundreds of undead approaching, against a backdrop of snow and the iconography of a community, is a striking one. ◇◇◇◇◇◇◇◇◇

2. **CITY SLICKERS**
After the carnage of 'All Out War,' issue 127 introduces us to a new world, set about two years in the future. Things have quite changed. Now, it appears our heroes are in control of the herd, not in fear of it. We witness Jesus, and others, all on horseback, steer a huge horde of walkers, just like their herding cattle, away from a new group of survivors. There's organization to it, too. They use horns and cattle-driving techniques to move the undead in whatever direction they wish. It's something we're not accustomed to seeing when it comes to the battle between the living and the dead. ◇◇◇◇◇◇◇

1. **A NEW ENEMY**
After the Negan war, things went a little quiet in *The Walking Dead*. There was even a country-style fair at one point. We mean, come on, it's all a bit civilized. Issue 143 changes that for good. Alpha, leader of the Whisperers, has Rick and Carl captive and wants to show our esteemed leader that she means business. Now, by this point, walkers have become the least of anyone's concerns, but if you amass a large enough quantity of any weapon it will become dangerous, and that's precisely what Alpha does. She takes Rick to the top of a four storey building and tells him to take a look over the edge – below are thousands of the things, all gathered in one small space. It might just be time to fear the walking dead again. •

NO WAY OUT

It's an all-action story, as Rick and the Alexandrians take on a huge herd of walkers in *Volume 14: No Way Out*. Although a linking story between two larger arcs, 'No Way Out' still features some important character developments and possibly one of the most shocking Charlie Adlard illustrations in the series' 10-year history. WORDS: Stuart Barr

I HOPE YOU'RE NOT TOO COMFORTABLE UP THERE...

Thomas Jefferson warned that "the price of freedom is eternal vigilance." In *Volume 14: No Way Out* we will discover that in an America unmade by the undead, eternal vigilance is the price of *survival*.

'No Way Out' is a transitional story bridging two larger narrative arcs. The first began with the fall of the prison (*Volume 8: Made To Suffer*) and ended with Rick Grimes and his group being brought into the Alexandria Safe-Zone. The second arc really begins in volume 15, as a series of interlocked stories opens up the world as we know it and the survivors of Alexandria seek to unite other communities against a mutual threat.

Never has a zombie attack been seen on this scale or duration as in 'No Way Out.' There is no other course of action but to fight.

Bridging stories can be unsatisfying, but Robert Kirkman ensures that this volume is packed with enough undead action to sustain interest, giving artist Charlie Adlard plenty of opportunity to splash the ink. *The Walking Dead* has featured siege stories before, but never has a zombie attack been seen of this scale or duration as it is in 'No Way Out.' As the title suggests, Rick is trapped with no other course of action but to fight.

Before this story starts, Rick and the other survivors have started to settle into Alexandria under the leadership of Douglas Monroe. However, they remain uncomfortable, unwilling to give up their firearms and coming into conflict with the Alexandrians. Douglas has fostered a semblance of pre-zombie life, but Rick's

group finds this artificial – perfectly illustrated later on when Michonne tells her 'retired' katana hanging on the wall: "I hope you're not too comfortable up there." Perhaps recognizing their discomfort, Monroe tried to integrate the newcomers into his community by giving them jobs. This delicately balanced house of cards has already begun to wobble, with allegations of sexual favoritism bringing repressed jealousies to light.

The volume opens with a crisis as scout Aaron rides into camp with boyfriend Eric slumped over his horse. The two are recruiters, tracking survivors and judging if they represent a useful addition

CLOP! CLOP! CLOP! CLOP! CLOP!

Douglas Monroe's delicately balanced house of cards has already begun to wobble, with allegations of sexual favoritism.

to the community – it was Aaron, for instance, who brought in Rick's group. Aaron tells Rick that they met a lone woman. She seemed harmless but during the night attacked Eric and stole his horse (actually Maggie Greene's horse, Buttons).

The incident is not only a reminder of the danger of trusting a stranger in these treacherous times, but also provokes (or rather doesn't) a strange post-event reaction in Maggie. Although she appears to have fully recovered from the depression that caused her attempted suicide (following the deaths of her father and brother at the prison), when Aaron tells her of the theft of her horse her reaction is simply unemotional; she even expresses relief that the animal is no longer penned. Maybe this is a healthy reaction to events, maybe she's just putting on a brave face, but Maggie has lost her entire family to the undead plague; given that the animal was her last link back to happier times, it is surprising she is not more upset.

Back to the action: Volume 13 ended in a gun battle between Alexandria residents and scavengers. The noise has drawn walkers to the walls. Sgt Abraham Ford shows his military training in trying to clear the walkers with his work detail, but matters escalate when a walker herd

OPPOSITE PAGE, TOP: Michonne's trusty katana won't be hung up for long! BOTTOM: Aaron and Eric ride back to the safety of Alexandria. THIS PAGE, TOP: Maggie is surprisingly calm about the loss of Buttons. ABOVE: The fences aren't holding up. ABOVE, RIGHT: Glenn and Heath face the enormity of the task ahead.

bears down on the community. Sheer volume of bodies makes retreat and entrenchment the only option. Unfortunately, crack-shot Andrea is left trapped in her sniper's nest atop the nearby clock tower outside the walls.

Rick calls a community meeting and calms panicked residents. His community address also allows Kirkman to provide some necessary exposition, making it clear that starvation is not a concern in the short term. What is a concern is ensuring the integrity of the walls. Rick delegates the task of inspecting and repairing the walls to Abraham's work detail, with Michonne taking the night watch. When Glenn raises Andrea's predicament, Rick is quick to evaluate that her situation is not immediately desperate.

One of the prime directives of Douglas Monroe's leadership regime was that no weapons were carried within the walls. Firearms were stored under lock and key. After the arrival of the herd, Rick rescinds that 'law,' reasoning that the circumstances are exceptional – notably, no-one objects. Even if he doesn't want the role, Rick is leading again, with Monroe sidelined.

As walkers crush against the community's walls, various

tensions arise between the inhabitants. With emotions running high, perhaps it's no surprise that passions are also enflamed, particularly between Michonne and Morgan, and Rick and Jessie Anderson. Neither of these relationships will end well...

In the previous volume, Rick had discovered that Jessie's husband was a wife-beater, leading the man to attempt to kill Rick, who defended himself with lethal force. Perhaps the extreme circumstances of this event leads Jessie to make romantic advances; perhaps she wants to give her son, Ron, a positive male role model. But whatever the truth, Rick responds in kind.

While their parents are otherwise occupied, Ron confronts Carl about Rick's killing of his father. Carl's reaction is matter-of-fact, effectively a "Yeah, what of it?" Carl tells Ron that both he and his father have killed out of necessity and faced by Carl's lack of regret and shame, Ron is left deflated. Ron is a child missing his daddy; Carl is above such childish feelings.

Michonne and Morgan are among the most 'damaged' characters in *The Walking Dead*. Michonne's history is sketchy, but we know she is emotionally distant and afraid of intimacy. We also know she had a daughter before the fall. Morgan lost his son, Duane, in circumstances that caused a psychological breakdown from which he is still very much in recovery. It is fitting that they find comfort in each other's arms. Michonne is corrective of Morgan's tendency for self-pity, while he humanizes her.

While on night patrol, Rick discovers part of the wall sagging. He discovers that, in places all around the community, the supporting beams for the fencing were sunk in packed dirt rather than cement. A necessity due to circumstances, of course, but under the illusion of safety created by Monroe's leadership it has resulted in a potential danger being forgotten – finding supplies of concrete and replacing the weak areas of the fence should have been a priority. Time and again it is clear that the greatest safety in *The Walking Dead* world is in community and numbers.

However, by trying to shut out the reality of the world outside their walls, the Alexandrians have created a ticking time bomb and the counter is approaching zero. Even as the walls sag, Tobin tries to convince Rick they will hold.

Glenn tells Rick he has an idea to take supplies to Andrea and draw away the herd, a daring plan to use a rope line to climb over the heads (and teeth) of the zombies to the clock tower. Although successful, the plan proves to be to no avail as the wall finally gives and the walkers pile into Alexandria. In the ensuing chaos, Tobin is quickly killed and Morgan bitten. Although Michonne rescues Morgan and quickly amputates his arm, she is too late and Morgan, rather unceremoniously, later ends his run in the series at the sharp end of Michonne's sword.

From their vantage point in the church tower, Glenn and Andrea watch on in horror as the herd swarms through the community. The situation becomes a desperate battle to escape the compound. Fractured into small groups hiding in buildings, all sense of community is lost. This is chillingly underlined when Jessie pleads with Rick to do something to save the children and he remarks, "The thing to keep in mind about other people's children... they're not our children."

Even so, Rick attempts to escape the compound with Jessie, Ron and Carl, this fails when Ron attracts attention and is bitten. Faced with overwhelming odds, even Rick panics and asks Jessie to leave her son to be consumed. In turn, she desperately clings to Carl and is herself dragged into the undead horde forcing Rick to hack off her hand to free his son.

Fearing all is lost, Monroe's last action is to stride into the mass of zombies, firing wildly with a handgun. He is quickly overwhelmed, but not before one of his stray bullets catches Carl in the head. Depicted in typically ruthless style and spread

> Even if he doesn't want the role, Rick is leading again, while Douglas has been sidelined.

YOUR DAD KILLED MY DAD...

AS WE GET TO THE MIDDLE... IT'S STARTING TO SAG MORE--WE SHOULD HAVE DONE THIS ONE AT A TIME.

Ron is a child missing his daddy; Carl is above such childish feelings.

OPPOSITE PAGE, LEFT: Andrea lays her sniper rifle aside as she's trapped in the clocktower. BOTTOM: Ron confronts Carl about his father's death at Rick's hands. THIS PAGE, ABOVE: Michonne takes drastic measures to try to save a bitten Morgan's life. RIGHT: Rick reminds Jessie that you can't look out for everyone in the walker apocalypse. BOTTOM: Glenn and Heath face danger as they go to the aid of a trapped Andrea.

...THEY'RE NOT *OUR* CHILDREN.

IN A NUTSHELL

TITLE: No Way Out
FEATURED ISSUES: 79-84
COLLECTION: Volume 14
SYNOPSIS: Drawn by the sound of gunfire, a gigantic herd of walkers descend on the Alexandria Safe-Zone. Initially stopped by the community's high walls, the walkers press up against the fencing and sheer numbers and some shoddy workmanship start to topple the walls. With the undead swarming through the streets, Rick is forced to flee, ending in disaster: Carl is shot through the eye by a wild bullet. With his son needing immediate medical attention, Rick has no choice but to stand and fight.

TIDBITS:

- Charlie Adlard had trouble finding suitable reference material for Carl's eye wound on the Internet, so had to 'invent' what has become one of the comic's most memorable and shocking images from scratch. Later, he received a photograph of a real person who had lived after receiving a similar gunshot wound to the head, proving the wound was survivable.

- Father Gabriel Stokes is given his chance for redemption in this volume. As we learned in *Volume 11: Fear The Hunters*, Gabriel had locked himself in his church when the walker outbreak began, refusing to let his parishioners in, effectively condemning them to death. This time, when desperate survivors come knocking on his door as the undead pour into Alexandria, he quickly opens it and ushers them inside.

- This volume marks the death of several key Alexandrians, including Jessie and Ron Anderson, Tobin and the community's former leader, Douglas Monroe. *TWDM* favorite Morgan Jones also meets his maker (blub!).

WE DON'T HAVE *TIME* FOR THAT--JUST KEEP MOVING. WE'VE ALREADY GOT TO WAIT FOR SPENCER. WHO KNOWS HOW LONG IT'LL TAKE US TO GET TO ANDREA IN THE TOWER.

I WANT TO GET THERE BEFORE DARK.

THUNK!

AAAGH!

LEFT: Jessie is left shocked (and dead) by Rick's actions. BELOW: This doesn't really need a caption, does it? BOTTOM LEFT: Andrea gets stuck in to protect Alexandria. BOTTOM RIGHT: Carl will never be the same again.

over two pages, Carl's shocked face, with destroyed right eye socket, and plaintive cry of "Dad?" remains one of the series' most brutal and memorable splash images. It is both shocking and emotionally charged. This is Rick's worst nightmare come true: despite his best efforts, Carl, his son, is on the verge of death.

After a frantic Rick carries the unconscious Carl to the community's doctor and begs her to save him, Rick and Michonne charge back into the fray, attacking the zombies with such savagery it inspires Abraham and others to join in.

Andrea and Glenn's group also mount a spirited offensive action against the horde outside the walls. In desperation, the fractured community slowly joins together again and despite the numerical superiority of the undead, the courage and resilience of the human survivors wins the day.

The story ends on one of *The Walking Dead*'s tensest cliffhangers, as Rick prays for Carl's life.

> Depicted in typically ruthless style, Carl's shot face remains one of the series' most brutal and memorable splashes.

WOW, YEAH...

Of course, readers of the comic will know Carl survives the event, albeit with a new scar, one which he cannot hide as easily as the bullet wound to his chest. As Negan says in issue 105: "I can see your fucking eye socket, your goddamn skull is exposed." Poor kid!

In conclusion, the moral and theme of the story is clear, Rick even declaims it in the final issue: strength is to be found in numbers and community. What is left unsaid is that the walls of

I WANT TO SHOW YOU THIS NEW WORLD. I WANT IT TO BE READY FOR YOU.

PLEASE, CARL--LIVE SO THAT I CAN SHOW YOU.

the Alexandria Safe-Zone fell despite this, predominantly because it was based on a flawed notion of community, one that tried not to keep the danger out, but to pretend the danger did not exist. As *The Walking Dead* (in all its numerous iterations) has shown time and time again, to forget the lethal nature of the world outside those walls, to lapse from a state of readiness, to fail to maintain "eternal vigilance" is to invite doom. •

CLASH OF THE TITANS

When giants of *The Walking Dead* meet, you can expect sparks to fly. This issue, Nicholas faces Glenn in a classic Mexican stand-off. **WORDS:** Dan Auty

WHAT'S THE BEEF?

Nicholas, Spencer, and Olivia aren't happy about the way Rick and his group have started to take over in Alexandria. Nicholas is planning to seize control – and this will inevitably involve killing Rick. Unfortunately, Glenn stumbles into the conversation and hears everything. His attempts to defuse the situation don't go down well with Nicholas when he sees that Glenn is holding a gun.

ROUND ONE!

Nicholas is straight in there, with a right hook to Glenn's jaw. Glenn goes down, but Nicholas keeps on pummeling him. Olivia manages to stop the attack, but Nicholas then picks up the gun and holds it to Glenn's bloodied head.

ROUND TWO!

Nicholas quickly discovers that Glenn – like all of Rick's group – has learned to survive without the safety of the walls the residents of Alexandria have grown accustomed to. Despite the gun at his head, Glenn hits

back, winding Nicholas and allowing him to escape. But the fight does not end there…

ROUND THREE!

Glenn races back and demands that Maggie gives him a gun. Meanwhile, a furious Nicholas and a larger group have gathered outside. Glenn emerges and a Mexican stand-off occurs, weapons pointed at each other, no one about to back down.

THE DECIDING BLOW

This is delivered not by Glenn or Nicholas, but by Rick, who steps into the situation

with his own gun, and tells Nicholas to give it up.

AND THE WINNER IS…

Glenn, with Rick's help. There's no knock-out, as Nicholas and the others slip away, back to their homes. But they now know that the authority that Rick and his group wield is far greater than their own.

THE SECRET DIARY OF A WALKER

It's not easy being a zombie in *The Walking Dead* world, as our week in the life/death of an undead walker reveals. Diary entries transcribed by Dan Auty.

MONDAY

It's my final week of training. The Mr Zombiverse competition takes place on Friday, and I need to get in shape. I like to start my morning with a long run through the woods, but my right foot dropped off over the weekend, and hobbling through the undergrowth isn't going to get me anywhere. Literally.

TUESDAY

Had a few questions today from other walkers about how I keep in such good shape. I tell them it's all about what's in the head. Not in my head, of course, that's a useless lump of bone. I mean the brains of all the normos I've been eating over the past few weeks.

WEDNESDAY

Went to check out some of my competition. I don't have much to worry about. Most of them could barely lift a single weight without snapping a limb, and the only thing strong about them is the smell.

THURSDAY

Final day of training. Bulking up as much as I can, but there's not much to eat round here – I did come across some normo lost in the woods, but there wasn't much to him. It's kinda pathetic that the normos haven't kept themselves in better shape. Would it have hurt to have saved a little more food in case there was, you know, a sudden zombie apocalypse?

FRIDAY

The big day! I won with no problem – my competition was basically some guy without legs, and a head with half a torso. Afterward, I thought I'd celebrate with a tasty treat and headed off into the woods again where I thought I heard someone moving around. Didn't expect to get a sword through my belly and see my guts all over the ground. Still, that's one way to lose the fat!

WORD
HE SAFE ZONES?

A man's home is his castle, as the saying goes. It should be a place of happiness, security, and shelter. Above all, it should be a safe place for all who live in it. But throw in the end of civilization and hundreds of thousands of flesh-hungry monsters and suddenly the place you once felt safest can become a horrible deathtrap. What you need instead is literally a castle, somewhere that is impregnable, defendable, and fit for habitation (providing a healthy source of food and water, for instance). It's a place that Rick, Carl, Michonne, and everyone else in *The Walking Dead* have been searching for, with limited success. With that in mind, *TWDM*'s resident health and safety inspector gives the series' various safe zones the once over to find out just how safe they really are.

WORDS: Nick Jones

THE CAMP

LOCATION: JUST OUTSIDE ATLANTA, GEORGIA

"So you're just camping out here? Is that safe?" asks Rick, appositely enough, when Glenn first leads him to the encampment on the scrubland outskirts of Georgia. To which Glenn responds that the band of happy campers have cars for shelter, that they take turns on watch at night, and that they "figure if we stick close to the city they'll be able to find us when the government sorts all this mess out." Before Rick can properly digest Glenn's threadbare assertions – and his touching faith in the competence of the federal authorities – he's distracted by the revelation that Lori and Carl, his wife and son, are alive and well, as is his best friend and fellow cop, Shane.

However, Rick's soon worrying away at Shane's determination to stay put, pointing out: "It's not smart to be this close to a city *full* of those things. It's just too *goddamn* dangerous." A few weeks later he's proved right when Amy's neck is ripped open by a roamer and Jim is bitten and dies shortly after. And then to cap it all, Carl goes and shoots Shane dead. It's enough to put a person off camping for life. Time to hit the road...

> WE ALL READY TO GO?

> I JUST NEED TO GET THE GAS FROM THE CARS INTO THE RV. WE'LL BE READY TO HIT THE ROAD AS SOON AS DALE'S READY.

> I'M ALL SET. WE CAN GO RIGHT AFTER WE'RE GASSED UP.

DEATH TOLL
-- BY WALKER: 2
-- BY HUMAN: 1

SAFETY RATING 5

WILTSHIRE ESTATES

LOCATION: 20 MILES FROM ATLANTA, GEORGIA

> I THINK WE'VE HIT THE JACKPOT.

"I think we've hit the jackpot," murmurs Rick to his fellow travelers upon arrival at the peaceful snowbound gated community of Wiltshire Estates, and then further seals the group's fate by declaring: "We should be relatively safe here."

Mind you, *relatively* speaking, they are, at least in terms of comparative body count: just the one death – the unfortunate Donna, chomped in the eye by a walker – as opposed to the three fatalities suffered at the Camp and the wholesale slaughter that lies in wait at future supposedly safe havens. But in truth, the writing was always on the wall for Wiltshire Estates – literally, in the form of a snow-covered sign warning "All Dead Do Not Enter," which, when Rick finally spies it, prompts a pithy rejoinder. Still, at least most of his group makes it out alive when the walker hordes make their presence known.

DEATH TOLL
-- BY WALKER: 1
-- BY HUMAN: 0

SAFETY RATING 4

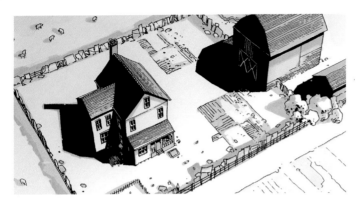

HERSHEL'S FARM

LOCATION: RURAL GEORGIA

Evidently, in the world of *The Walking Dead*, the word 'safe' is anything but a safe word. Case in point: Hershel Greene's farm, which actually looks quite promising as a haven — plenty of food and plenty of room, too — until Hershel informs Rick that "during the day you won't have to worry about being safe." Nnnnoooo — don't say that!

Ah, but it's too late: no sooner has Hershel uttered the 'S' word than he's telling Rick not to go in the barn: "That's where we keep all our dead ones." Of course you do, Hershel. Needless to say, it's not long before those nearest, dearest, and deadest are inadvertently set free, resulting in the gruesome demise of two members of the Greene clan (one of them at the zombified hands — or rather teeth — of his own brother). Unsurprisingly, Rick and co are soon on the road again.

DEATH TOLL	SAFETY RATING
-- BY WALKER: **2**	**5**
-- BY HUMAN: **0**	

DEATH TOLL	SAFETY RATING
-- BY WALKER: **5**	**3**
-- BY HUMAN: **14**	

THE PRISON

LOCATION: MERIWETHER COUNTY, RURAL GEORGIA

As is becoming abundantly clear, if any of *The Walking Dead* character utters the word 'safe' in connection with any kind of haven, you can be damn sure the place will eventually prove to be anything but. So when, upon first setting eyes on the Meriwether County Correctional Facility, Rick rolls out the 'safe' word not once but *three* times, he effectively dooms the place there and then.

Still, for a short while at least, the Prison does appear to be, as Rick also puts it, "perfect" — that is, if you ignore the fact that it's riddled with walkers and boasts a quartet of deeply suspicious inmates — and when folks do start dying it's initially mostly by human hand (a bungled suicide pact, a serial killer, impromptu executions, and so on).

However, when Rick and co visit Woodbury and the Governor becomes aware of the Prison's existence, the correctional facility's fate is sealed, and after a deceptive period of calm, the Governor and his army attack. Tyreese is the first to go — beheaded by the Governor — swiftly followed by another half-dozen of Rick's group, including Lori and her child, as the fences come down and the Prison is overrun by Woodbury soldiers and rampant roamers.

Oh well. It was nice (well, as nice as prisons get anyway) while it lasted — and it lasted longer than most.

WOODBURY

LOCATION: GEORGIA

Prior to Rick, Michonne, and Glenn's arrival at the place, you could argue that the citizens of Woodbury had it pretty good. Sure, the guy in charge, the self-styled Governor, might be a Grade-A psychopath who keeps his zombified niece as a pet and collects severed heads in aquariums. And yes, there was always the possibility of ending up in the arena fighting for your life surrounded by chained walkers. But hey, at least there was free entertainment on offer!

Rick et al's arrival puts paid to all that, however – at least we assume so, since we've yet to see what became of Woodbury itself in the comic book (although you can find out in the novel series). Certainly for many of its denizens, though, getting mixed up with Rick's group turns out to be *a very bad* idea, chiefly when the Governor leads his army against the Prison and his soldiers are slaughtered by the jail's defenders – or, in the case of the Governor himself, by his own troops.

DEATH TOLL
-- BY WALKER: **1**
-- BY HUMAN:
Dozens of Woodbury soldiers and denizens

SAFETY RATING
2

FATHER GABRIEL'S CHURCH

LOCATION: VIRGINIA

For the Prison survivors it's a long, hard road to their next (supposedly) safe haven, with numerous perils including walker herds and marauding bandits, although they do make new acquaintances along the way in the shape of Abraham, Rosita, and Eugene, and get reacquainted with Morgan (whose own humble haven for himself and his son, Duane, has turned out to be far from safe: Duane is now a walker, whom Morgan keeps on a chain). They also meet Father Gabriel Stokes, who leads them to his church, which he suggests "could offer the sanctuary you're looking for."

A different 'S' word, but in the backstory of the church, the same unfortunate connotations, as Gabriel reveals that when the zombie plague started, he locked the doors of his "sanctuary" and left his "neighbors, friends… members of my congregation" to die outside.

The grounds of the church also prove to be the final resting place for one of Rick's group: Dale, who

finally succumbs to a walker bite and the wounds he received at the hands of the Hunters. But that's really the only death that can be linked to the church, and even then only loosely, making the House of Gabriel's God one of the safest places thus far. Er, unless you count Gabriel's former flock…

DEATH TOLL
-- BY WALKER: **1**
(or loads, depending on how far back you go)
-- BY HUMAN: **0**

SAFETY RATING
6

THE ALEXANDRIA SAFE-ZONE

LOCATION: SOUTH OF WASHINGTON, DC, VIRGINIA

On the face of it, the walled community of the Alexandria Safe-Zone must surely rank as one of the safest havens of all. After all, at time of writing, it's still going strong and Rick and at least some of his group are still in residence. But try telling that to all those poor swine who have lost their lives since Rick and his group arrived.

In retrospect, the warning signs were there right from the start. When Alexandria resident Aaron first tells Rick about his homestead, not only does Rick use the 'safe' word in conjunction with this unseen promised land, he adds another 'S' word: "secure" – and Aaron doesn't help matters when he claims his community is "completely safe." But there is admittedly an extended period at Alexandria where nobody dies – until Rick tackles a case of domestic violence and winds up with a couple of corpses on his hands, and then the place is attacked by scavengers.

LITTLE PIG, LITTLE PIG.

LET ME IN.

Even so, Alexandria does prove a safe refuge from roamers… Right up until the point the walls come tumbling down and the place is overrun by walkers, putting paid to Rick's new beau, Jessie, and her son (among others), and leaving Carl with a gaping hole in his head.

But that's as nothing compared to the all-out war that erupts with Negan and his Saviors. First to die is Abraham, then Glenn, then a traitorous Spencer, then Eric, Holly, Denise (chomped by a zombified Holly), and a bunch more in Negan's assault on Alexandria (including the entire Orson family). By the time it's all over, more than a dozen Alexandrians have lost their lives.

'Safe-Zone?' Hmm, not so much…

All that being said, Alexandria does have one big plus in its favor as a safe haven: for two years following the war with Negan, peace and relative prosperity reign, and in the violent world of *The Walking Dead*, two years is a considerable length of time. Naturally, that period of calm is brought to a bloody conclusion when the Whisperers arrive on the scene and murder another half dozen or so Alexandrians…

DEATH TOLL
-- BY WALKER: **8**
-- BY HUMAN: **22**

} SAFETY {
} RATING {
-- ON LONGEVITY: **9**
-- ON LIVES LOST: **2**
-- OVERALL:

7

THE HILLTOP LOCATION: VIRGINIA

WE'RE HERE.

WELCOME TO THE HILLTOP.

Now, you could argue that the single factor which unites all of the havens and zones examined thus far, in regard to their decline in status from safe to really-not-so-safe, is, well, Rick. Anyone attempting to make such a case need look no further than Rick's arrival at the Hilltop for evidence: within minutes he's slashed the throat of one of its residents (admittedly in self-defense). But the Saviors and the Whisperers can't be blamed on Rick (not entirely anyway), and it's they who are responsible for most of the Hilltop's deaths (largely the result of Negan's fence-smashing assault and Alpha and the Whisperers' off-campus beheadings). Apart from Gregory's death, of course. He's strung up on the orders of Rick's protégé, Maggie. Ahem!

DEATH TOLL
-- BY WALKER: **0**
-- BY HUMAN:
   More than a dozen

| SAFETY | RATING |

6

WRA

THE SANCTUARY
LOCATION: VIRGINIA

The Sanctuary itself is a formidable proposition as a safe-zone: a factory surrounded by a fence and protected by walkers and barricades. But that's without factoring in Negan, who sends his men to deadly defeat after deadly defeat. Indeed, so many Saviors are 'offed' during the course of Negan's war on Alexandria, the Hilltop, and the Kingdom that it's a wonder there are any left alive at the end of it all. Add in a few victims of Alpha and the Whisperers and, well, the death toll below says it all.

DEATH TOLL
-- BY WALKER: 1
-- BY HUMAN: **Somewhere around 75**

SAFETY RATING
-- AS A PLACE, A SOLID 8
-- FOR ITS UNFORTUNATE DENIZENS: 1
-- OVERALL:

5

THE KINGDOM
LOCATION: DISTRICT OF COLUMBIA

Of all the major zones — Alexandria, the Hilltop, and the Sanctuary — the Kingdom has a good claim on being the most secure of the lot. An abandoned high school, for protection it boasts a metal wall, a second wall of school buses and, best of all, an actual, living, no-kidding tiger. Even its death toll is comparatively low, although that number does eventually include its self-styled king, Ezekiel, and his aforementioned tiger, Shiva.

On balance, though, the Kingdom seems about the soundest haven yet seen in *The Walking Dead*, and therefore is hereby declared the zone supreme. At least until someone declares it as being 'safe'…

DEATH TOLL
-- BY WALKER: 1 tiger
-- BY HUMAN: More than a dozen

SAFETY RATING
8

TOP 5

SAFE AS HOUSES! Top Five Safe Zones

JAILHOUSE ROCK

Until that nasty Governor guy brought an army of tanks, trucks, and ammunition with him, the prison had proved itself to be a real safe haven. To date, it's arguably the most fortified of all the safe zones in *The Walking Dead,* and for that reason, it makes our top five. Let's face it, layers of barbed wire fencing, several watchtowers, from which our heroes could scout the land, and a raft of munitions and armor readily available made it a very safe place to be. The walkers couldn't break its walls and our heroes felt so safe they even started to grow their own fruit and veg.

4. A WALK ON THE WILD SIDE

The Alexandria Safe-Zone has to make this top five; but it's also the site of *The Walking Dead*'s fiercest walker invasion. Hundreds of the ugly things break down the walls and overrun the place, turning what was

once a seemingly secure place into somewhere no better than hell. There are casualties aplenty, including Rick's new love interest, Jessie, and her son, Ron. Following Rick's lead, they cake themselves in zombie guts and traipse after the gang in an effort to evade the horde. Unfortunately, they're both devoured. To add to the misery, Carl gets shot in the eye, when a stray bullet hits him instead of a biter.

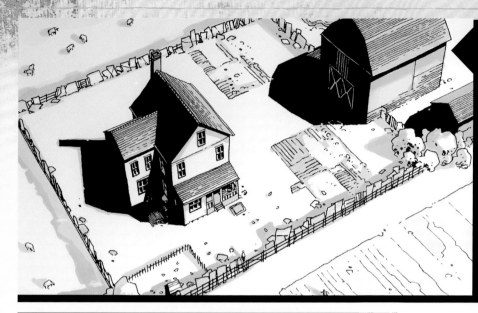

3. HOME FROM HOME

After more than 100 days on the road, our heroes are weary and worn, and in need of some home comforts. So, despite the means by which they find the place (as a result of young Carl Grimes getting shot), their winding up at the Greene family farm is extremely welcome. For that reason, it makes the top five list of safe zones. After all, it's the first time, after learning that the world has gone to crap, that our heroes are reminded of what once was and what they want, more than anything else, again.

2. GROUND ZERO

The Hilltop makes the list because it's where the war between the Saviors and, to be frank, everyone else, reaches its bloody conclusion. The series' most despotic villain, Negan, orders his men to smash down the colony's gates and kill everyone and everything in sight, and that's what they set about doing. Armed with weapons smeared in zombie mulch, the Saviors storm the town, killing and maiming whoever they come into contact with. But after being outflanked by Rick, Negan is captured and imprisoned. Quite a moment in the series. ◇◇◇◇◇◇

1. NO SANCTUARY

While we don't spend an awful lot of time getting to know the Sanctuary – the home of the Saviors – the place certainly leaves its mark. Primarily, that's because of its people and their mostly unwavering devotion to their crazy-ass leader. They jump at his every word, like he's Julius Caesar or something. The Sanctuary is also where Carl gets an insight into the mind of Negan, one of the comic's most compelling characters. Interestingly, the former factory is surrounded by a wall of walkers, impaled on poles – a means of keeping away more of the horrible things, no doubt. ◇◇◇◇◇◇◇◇◇

WE FIND OURSELVES

Anatomy of a Story takes a look at the volume which follows the walker invasion of Alexandria – *Volume 15: We Find Ourselves.* It's a less action-packed storyline, instead focusing much more on an introspective Rick and his development into a *bona fide* leader, from his relationship with his son to the future of Alexandria.

WORDS: Stuart Barr

Rick's romantic life is about to have a major development that would be impossible to replicate in the show.

The season six mid-season cliffhanger ended with Rick and a group, including Jessie and Ron Anderson, attempting to escape from a walker-besieged house by covering themselves in gore to fool the undead. This happened toward the end of volume 14, but the comic continues to a drastic dénouement after the point 'Start To Finish' cut to its credits. A terrified Ron cried out, alerting the walkers, and was dragged into the herd. Jessie would not let go of her son or of Carl, threatening to drag Rick's son into the feeding frenzy too. To save his boy, Rick hacked off Jessie's arm with his trusty axe, thus dooming the Andersons to a horrible fate. The survivors then rallied and fought off the walker incursion. However, in the chaos, Carl was hit by a stray bullet that took off a chunk of his face and caused him to lose his right eye.

As the time of writing this article, the mid-season premiere was

Alexandria has become a fractured community desperately in need of hope and leadership.

Volume 15 of *The Walking Dead* marks the transition from the previous Alexandria Safe-Zone storyline, which focused on Rick's group being recruited and assimilated into the survivor community, to the introduction of the Saviors, which comes into full effect in volume 16's 'A Larger World.' At the end of volume 14 ('No Way Out' – interestingly also the title of season six's mid-season premiere episode), a walker herd had broken through the walls of the Alexandria settlement causing widespread carnage, which was dramatized in the season six episode 'Start to Finish'.

There are some important differences between the two to note. In the comic, Andrea is alive and well while Morgan Jones is very much the opposite. Carl Grimes' TV incarnation has long since deviated from the comic for practical reasons – actor Chandler Riggs has grown up over six years of filming – and baby Judith is but a sad memory, having died in her mother's arms at the prison, some 30 issues previously. As such, the comic's storyline cannot be fully replicated in the TV series; for instance, in this storyline,

GOOD EFFORT, EVERYONE-- BUT SAVE YOUR BULLETS.

I'LL TAKE IT FROM HERE.

Rick is a worried parent facing the death of his child. He may be a leader, but with this situation, he is utterly powerless.

about to air, so we don't know if events followed the comic book exactly, but the details that we do know suggest that many of the twists in this tale will see the light of day in the show. Jessie, Ron, and Sam (a character unique to the show) look somewhat doomed, with the frightened Sam beginning to crack under the pressure of the monsters all around him. Carl being shot was perhaps the big shocker, especially as Robert Kirkman recently noted in *The Walking Dead Magazine*: "It's not necessarily the logistics of the CGI that dictates what the story

focus is or what we lose, but having a main character who has lost a hand or an eye would lead to a lot of problems." Well, surprise!

Anyway, back to the comic. Volume 15 begins with the clean up of the aftermath of the Alexandria invasion. Abraham Ford finds and dispatches the now zombified Jessie (with the hand Rick hacked off still attached by rotting sinew). Rick is in the

infirmary with a comatose Carl. Guilt-ridden, Rick describes what happened to Jessie and Ron while a horrified Denise Cloyd listens on. It is not clear if Rick is really aware of Denise's presence in the room. She is clearly shaken by what she hears, something that explains her inaction later in the volume.

A series of character vignettes give an overview of key relationships in the community. Spencer Monroe is still pursuing Andrea, but it is clear she has no interest in him any more. Maggie and Glenn seem happy, but she confesses that being content makes her feel bad. Glenn ascribes this to 'survivor guilt.' Abraham and Rosita have hit the rocks; Abraham has been cheating on her with Alexandria native Holly, and Rosita reveals she knows about the affair before moving in with a stunned Eugene. Abraham's later attempts to apologize are ham-fisted and patronizing, enraging Rosita even further.

These short scenes paint a picture of a fractured community desperately in need of hope and leadership. Rick holds a community meeting, admitting he has been approaching the concept of survival all wrong. He recognizes that real safety is in numbers and wants to build something in Alexandria – a self-sustaining settlement. This realization also features in the TV series and will inform much of the rest of season six.

Later, when Andrea checks on Rick and Carl, Rick reveals his

Scavenging farther afield leads to its own problems: the danger level increases exponentially as the group forages farther away from Alexandria.

IN A NUTSHELL

TITLE: We Find Ourselves
FEATURED ISSUES:
#85 to 90
COLLECTION: Volume 15
SYNOPSIS: Following the invasion of Alexandria by a huge walker herd, Rick is forced to face his fears over losing the most precious thing in his life, Carl. His son's horrific injury, caused by a gunshot to the head, forces Rick to reassess what survival really means. It is not enough just to survive – he and the rest of the Alexandrians must learn to live again. His best chance of saving his son is to build a community that can resist not just the walkers, but all of life's other obstacles. He is learning to fight not just for his life or that of his son, but also for the group. With Negan and the Saviors on the horizon, this crucial turning point in Rick's outlook will become ever more important as the story progresses.

TIDBITS:

- Rick's confrontation with the conspiratorial Nicholas was almost word-for-word replicated in season six's premiere, 'First Time Again,' with Carter taking the Nicholas role (and without the swearing!).

- No major characters die in this issue, unless you count Abraham killing an undead Jessie.

- A funeral is held for those killed in the walker herd invasion, as seen in the last volume, namely: Jessie, Ron, Douglas, Tobin, and Morgan. This is the second Alexandria funeral we've seen in the comic to date, following Pete's burial in issue #78 (the same issue that Douglas decided to make Rick the community's leader).

Rick realizes that living in the moment has made them vulnerable. He has been neglecting long-term survival strategies to the detriment of everyone.

fear that his son will die. As if on cue, Carl shows signs of life without regaining consciousness just yet. Denise sees it as a positive sign, but tries to manage Rick's expectations about Carl's recovery prospects. Rick is a worried parent facing the death of his child… again! He may be the leader, he may be making wide-ranging plans on behalf of the community, but in this situation, he is utterly powerless.

Denise insists that Rick goes home to rest. Reluctantly walking home, Rick comes across Michonne kneeling by Morgan Jones's grave. She tells him she wasn't kind to Morgan, but that he had made her try to be better. Comparing her dysfunctional relationship to Rick and Jessie's, Michonne asks, "What is wrong with us?" She may be well-meaning and even truthful, but Rick doesn't need to hear this right now. In contrast, his deepening friendship with Andrea is more positive. She reinforces his best qualities and her advice is nearly always good.

There is trouble brewing elsewhere, however. Nicholas, a discontented Alexandrian, is sowing dissent among the community's established residents. His position gains traction when it's revealed food supplies are running low, even with a suddenly depleted population. With winter just beginning, rationing will be a necessity unless supplies are replenished soon. With scavenging nearby leading to gradually diminishing returns, it's clear that the search radius must be extended. But that in turn leads to its own problems: the danger level increases exponentially as the group forages farther afield, away from the safety of Alexandria.

On the plus side, Rick is urgently summoned to the infirmary, where he finds Carl is waking up. Tense moments pass as Rick waits for Carl to speak, worried his son may have permanent brain damage. Carl's first word is simply, "Dad." Good news.
His next are, "Where's mom?" Not so good.

Rick's role as a loving parent is tempered by his position as the *de facto* leader of the community.

Rick is devastated. Carl seems to be recovering, but his memory gaps mean his father faces the prospect of having to "break his heart" continually if his memory cannot retain the information that Lori has died. The next day, he takes decisive action on this dilemma and tells Carl his mother is dead. The boy's reaction is unexpected – he is not cold exactly, but neither is he distressed. Rick explains that Lori died with his infant sister, Judith, but Carl cannot remember either. Rick asks him, "Are you sad?" and he replies in the negative; he cannot remember his mother's death, but she does not feel present to him. So, Carl cannot remember the specific events, but he has an awareness that his mother is gone. Is this really a memory loss issue? Perhaps he is suppressing traumatic memories while still in recovery. Carl also remembers Ron and Jessie were attacked and died, but again, he doesn't remember specific details.

Rick puts an end to the Alexandrian rebellion, but perhaps surprisingly doesn't kill ringleader Nicholas. Prison-era Rick would have killed him on the spot.

Rick's role as a loving parent is tempered by his position as the *de facto* leader of the community following previous leader Douglas Monroe's death in the walker herd invasion. As such, Rick organizes a party to venture beyond the walls to scout for supplies. Denise thinks he is using this as a way to avoid talking to Carl. Is he afraid that he will have to explain Lori's death to him over and over again, or that Carl will suddenly remember the details of Ron and Jessie's deaths?

During the patrol (which, as anticipated, recovers almost nothing), Rick finds a quiet spot and weeps under the weight of recent events. Andrea finds him and he reveals his real fear about Carl: "What good is keeping him alive... if I've lost my little boy?" Is this an extreme form of empty nest syndrome?

Back at Alexandria, Nicholas continues his insurrection against Rick. Olivia doesn't "necessarily" agree that they will be safer without the newcomers, but she also doesn't actively try to stop

Nicholas. Rick's confession about Ron and Jessie is no doubt the reason for her reluctance.

Nicholas announces he wants Rick dead and, naturally, this is precisely when Glenn stumbles onto the scene. He tries to back away from a confrontation, but Nicholas is too far gone. Glenn escapes, running to warn Maggie to take Sophia to safety. Nicholas follows him, gunning for blood, but is stopped by Heath. As Nicholas is raving about taking Alexandria back, he fails to notice Rick's return.

Rick quickly puts an end to the rebellion, but perhaps surprisingly doesn't kill Nicholas, instead telling him that he is needed to make Alexandria safe again. Prison-era Rick would have killed him on the spot, but he now has new priorities.

When Carl is well enough to return home, Rick must once again take on his role as a parent. Carl asks his father whether he would have been sad if he had died. Rick is aghast. Carl says he knows Rick

Rick realizes that his default reaction when his group is threatened is to kill, and it has left him feeling emotionally dead.

loves him, but that he is also so strong. This almost exactly mirrors Rick's fears about his son. Both are afraid that the other's strength makes them psychologically resistant to emotion. Carl tells his father he is remembering more about Lori and is beginning to feel sad, and that he has been afraid that this is a weakness. This moment marks an emotional change in Carl, which will come out much more in the volumes to follow; he is no longer Rick's little boy.

Later, after Carl is asleep, Rick and Andrea talk and Rick reveals he wanted to kill Nicholas. He recognizes that this had become his default reaction when his group is threatened and it has left him feeling emotionally dead. Andrea disagrees that he is a lost cause and the volume ends with them falling into an embrace.

As the title of this volume suggests, Rick has come to realize that living only in the moment, focusing only on survival, has made them vulnerable. He has been neglecting longer-term survival strategies to the detriment of everyone around him. The ever-present threat of mortality makes it difficult to find rational solutions. Rick now truly believes that 'the group' is the best protection. This notion is reinforced throughout the volume and is crucial to the coming Saviors storyline. Faced with a threat like Negan, it would be easy to take flight. Rick needs a reason to stay and fight, to risk his family, his friends, and his community for an ideal. Alexandria is that ideal. •

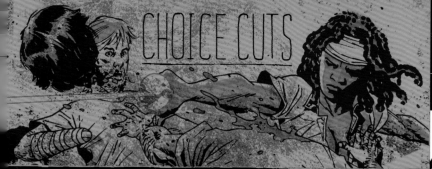

THE CHILDREN OF *THE WALKING DEAD*

The Walking Dead Magazine goes a little deeper into who the leading child characters in the comic are, selecting their crowning moments and worst deeds. WORDS: Dan Auty

> I DON'T THINK SO. I MISS MOM, BUT EVEN THOUGH I DON'T REMEMBER... IT DOESN'T FEEL LIKE SHE'S ALIVE. SHE FEELS... GONE.

> I DON'T REMEMBER JUDY. IT'S SAD THAT SHE'S DEAD... BUT MOST EVERYONE I KNOW IS DEAD. I REMEMBER AMY DIED. I LIKED HER. AND SOPHIA'S MOM DIED. TYREESE DIED. MORGAN DIED, AND...

> ...JESSIE AND RON DIED, TOO...

CARL

Carl is the youngster who we've followed most closely from the very start of *The Walking Dead*. While adult characters are clearly affected by their experiences and changed by the world around them, they are nevertheless grown-ups who have reached adulthood with their outlooks and attitudes fully formed. Carl, however, grows from a normal seven-year-old, relying almost entirely on his parents, to an assured, self-sufficient, old-before-his-years teenager.

Carl has had to deal with the tragic loss of both his mother and baby sister, and the moment that he was accidentally shot through the face by Douglas Monroe in issue 83 was a defining one. At first, Carl attempts to hide the disfigurement,

> OH...

wrapping it in bandages. But an encounter with Negan – who tells him he looks "F**king rad" – prompts him to leave it uncovered, simply wearing his hair long to conceal the wound.

By the time we leap forward two years, Carl is wearing glasses with a blacked-out eyepiece. But finally Lydia persuades him that he should have no fear of letting the world see his whole face. As his confidence and survival abilities have grown, so has the realization that his physical appearance is part of who he is – and anyone who doesn't like it just has to deal with it.

SOPHIA

Like Carl, Sophia has survived throughout the entire run of the comic. Her mother Carol died in the most gruesome way possible – offering herself to a walker – after which Sophia was adopted by Maggie and Glenn. Her bond with Maggie grows so strong that she begins to act as if she really is her mother. So much so, that Carl confronts her about this behavior, claiming she is in denial about what happened to her real mother. When Maggie returns from a mission to find supplies, the 10-year-old makes it clear that she knows exactly what's going on. "You know I'm just pretending," she tells Maggie. "I'm not so scared anymore, so I can talk about that now."

Sophia is still alive to this day in the comic, and her bond with both Maggie and Carl remains as strong as ever. When Sophia was attacked by two Hilltop boys, Carl leapt to her defense, seriously injuring them in retaliation. She may not be his girlfriend anymore, but no one messes with a friend of the Grimes boys.

THE GREENE TWINS

Hershel's twin teenage daughters, Rachel and Susie, didn't make it past issue 15, and didn't really play that big a part of the ongoing storyline until the very end. But their demise at the hands of Thomas Richards was important, because it showed that Robert Kirkman and Charlie Adlard were just as prepared to dish out gruesome treatment to kids as they were to the adults. Just because they are children, doesn't mean they wouldn't get their head chopped off by a homicidal psychopath. As shocking as this moment is, it did not stop us being shocked to the core by baby Judith's death some 30 issues later.

BEN AND BILLY

Rachel and Susie aren't *The Walking Dead*'s only twins. Allen and Donna's twin boys, Ben and Billy, were much younger, and still naïve about the world around them. After the death of their parents, they were adopted by Dale and Andrea.

Their story climaxes in a disturbing scene in which Ben kills his brother, the five-year-old's mental deterioration leading him to believe that no real harm has been done since the dead always return. "I didn't hurt his brains," he tells a horrified Andrea.

This tragedy also provides Carl with another defining moment. With Ben locked in Dale's trailer and the adults in the group in disagreement about what to do with him, Carl takes the initiative. He sneaks out of his tent while Rick is asleep, enters the trailer and shoots Ben dead. Only Morgan knows what really happened, and he keeps quiet about it.

GIVE DADDY A KISS.

PENNY

Plenty of kids have died throughout the course of *The Walking Dead*, but Penny Blake is the only one who starts her time in the comic already deceased. Penny is the niece of the Governor. He refuses to let his zombified relative go, and keeps her chained up in his Woodbury house, bringing her buckets of human meat and removing her teeth so he can give her big, sloppy kisses. Lucky kid!

DUANE JONES

Penny is not the only zombie kid we've seen in the comic. Who can forget Morgan's child, Duane? When Rick returns to his hometown, he discovers that a half-mad Morgan has been attacking unwary travelers and feeding them to his zombified son. Urging Morgan to do the right thing and put his child out of his misery, Rick passes him a gun. Rick then takes his friend away with him, not knowing that Morgan actually shot the chain holding his son prisoner rather than put the bullet through his brain.

What makes this moment even more poignant is that we first met Duane when he was very much alive, surviving

BILLY GREENE

Billy was Hershel's youngest son, and despite his youth – he was barely 18 – ultimately proved to be one of the most useful members of the team.

Andrea is quick to identify his skill with firearms, and realizing that he is the second-best shot in the group, she and Rick make the most of his talents. Billy's greatest moment comes during the Governor's final assault on the prison, when he becomes a one-man army, blasting away from his sniper's perch, while liberally tossing grenades at the advancing enemies. Sadly, he only makes it to the next issue before he is himself killed in the battle. Unlike many, he goes out in some glory.

THEY'RE HERE!

PTING!

TING!

GRAHHGH.

with his dad just as Rick and Carl have been up to Rick and Morgan's reunion. Morgan clearly failed to protect Duane sometime between issues 1-58 and feels so guilty about not saving his son's life, he now can't bear the thought of ending it permanently, even if it was probably the 'decent' thing to do.

JULIE AND CHRIS

True love rarely runs smoothly in the world of *The Walking Dead*, and nowhere is this more true than for teenage lovers Julie and Chris. The pair were together when the zombie apocalypse began, but Chris in particular seemed ill-equipped to deal with this harsh new world.

After frequently complaining to Rick that he wasn't being treated as an adult in the prison, Chris made the decision that the only way he and Julie could be together forever would be a joint suicide pact. Unfortunately, his flawed plan involved them shooting each other simultaneously, and Julie was killed before she could pull the trigger on him. Luckily, Julie's dad, Tyreese, was on hand to finish the job for him, first strangling Chris in an anguish-fuelled rage. "He'll be coming back soon, and I'm gonna kill him again," Tyreese spits. "Slower this time."

RON

The difference between Carl and many other children is clearly shown in a short exchange with Ron Anderson, the son of Pete, the wife-beating husband of Jessie, whom Rick kills soon after the group's arrival in Alexandria. While few mourn Pete – least of all Jessie – Ron finds it hard to process his death. He knows that Pete wasn't a nice man, but he was still his father and he loved him. It was for that reason alone that Rick agrees to give Pete a funeral.

When Jessie and Ron come to stay in Rick's house, Ron goes into Carl's room, late at night, looking for some answers. "Your dad killed my dad," he tells him. "Why's your dad get to be good but my daddy is bad?" Carl's answer is blunt in the way that only someone who has had to survive on the outside for a long time could be: "I don't know. It's just how things are."

Ron dies a few issues later, clinging to his mother as they are both devoured by walkers.

WHY'S YOUR DAD GET TO BE *GOOD* BUT MY DADDY IS *BAD?*

I DON'T KNOW.

IT'S JUST HOW THINGS *ARE.*

JOSH

While Carl and Lydia begin to form something vaguely resembling a normal teenage relationship, the fate of Josh at the hands of Lydia's mother is a stark reminder that such things aren't really possible.

Josh is a friend of Carl's in the post-time jump Alexandria, and while their friendship formed over the two years we didn't see, they have become close. The discovery of Josh's severed head on a post, planted with 11 others by Alpha to mark the boundary between the Whisperers and the community, hits Carl hard.

"I haven't lost a friend in a long time," the teenager tells Lydia sadly.

LYDIA

As Carl grows older, it's no surprise that he starts to take an interest in members of the opposite sex. While Sophia has really just been a friend over the years (a pre-pubescent girlfriend, at best), Lydia is something much more. As a member of the flayed-skin-wearing Whisperers, she is initially set up as a villain, but during her time as the Hilltop's prisoner, we see that she is as much a victim as any of the Whisperers' prey.

The scenes between Lydia and Carl reveal her fear about being returned to her people, and how she has been systematically abused by the men of the group, all with her mother's silent approval. The time spent in the Hilltop has made Lydia realize that the Whisperers' brutal way of doing things is not the only path to survival.

CARL, IS THAT YOU?

"I just thought that was the way things were, Carl," she says. "You're showing me another way."

That was the first indication that Lydia is attracted to Carl. She's a lot clearer shortly after. Climbing on top of him, she asks whether he's ever had sex. Carl is too shocked to answer, but when Lydia then asks him whether he would like to be with her, he manages to reply "Okay!" The boy has finally become a man…

CLASH OF THE TITANS

When giants of *The Walking Dead* meet, you can expect sparks to fly... Carl and Sophia take on two Hilltop bullies, Brandon and Harlan. **WORDS:** Dan Auty

WHAT'S THE BEEF?

This particular altercation is the payoff to an earlier conflict. Two bullies – Brandon and Harlan – had previously picked on Brian in issue 131. That didn't go well for the pair, with Sophia stepping in to defend her friend and quickly dispatching the bullies. Revenge is on their mind, and poor Carl finds himself on the receiving end of it when they see him and Sophia sitting quietly together.

ROUND ONE!

It's a dirty blow – Brandon sneaks up behind Carl and hits him on the back of his

head with a brick. Carl falls to the ground, then runs off, leaving Sophia to face the two bullies alone, who promise her "things will be different this time!"

ROUND TWO!

Sophia is one tough kid. Despite being outnumbered, she swings at Brandon and lands a hard punch on his

jaw. But it's two against one, and soon the boys are beating her senseless.

ROUND THREE!

Carl is back! With a loud 'SHUKK!', he whacks Harlan round the cranium with a shovel. Blow after blow reigns down on the kid, before the furious Carl turns to deliver the same treatment to Brandon.

THE DECIDING BLOW

To Sophia's horror, Carl strikes Brandon again and again with the shovel. The fight is over as quickly as it began. But at what cost?

AND THE WINNER IS...

Carl clearly won this one, but his look of blank terror when we see him next, staggering with Sophia back to Maggie, says it all. "I think I killed them," he mutters.

The bullies are not dead, luckily, but Carl's actions have considerable consequences for him, his family, and his friends in the story to come. •

THE SECRET DIARY OF A WALKER

It's not easy being a zombie in *The Walking Dead* world, as our week in the life/death of an undead walker reveals. Diary entries transcribed by Stuart Barr.

MONDAY

Went out for a run. It's cold out, so got my hoodie zipped up. Keeping up my cardio work – it always surprises the mouth-breathers when you can chase 'em. Funny, sometimes nerdy ones in horror movie T-shirts complain about 'fast zombies' – just before I bite through their carotids. Should have hit

the gym instead of standing in line for the Halloween horror maze, guys!

TUESDAY

Since I died, my lap times have been shocking. On the upside, I don't need to hydrate and I never get cramps. However, I do admit the worst thing about being dead is the lack of coordination. But

I've been practicing and I haven't run into a streetlight all week. Running does get my blood flowing though – at least, I think it's still blood.

WEDNESDAY

It's lonely being an undead track bunny. Since Rotten Ronald got his lower intestine caught on the starting block trying to sprint the 100m and ripped his bowels out, none of the guys have been interested in working out.

THURSDAY

Disaster! Was in the zone, powering along the highway and didn't notice I'd run into the woods. Now I can't find my way out. Getting hungry. I've seen mouth-breathers sneaking around in the trees. I'm going to try to sneak up on them. Need the protein.

FRIDAY

I'm in luck – a lot of mouth-breathers are out shouting "Dale!" I dunno who this Dale is, but I'm in the mood for some brains – a better energy boost than a whole box of PowerZoom bars. They're coming this way. I think I'll just hide in this bush... •

TOP 5

BAD PARENTING GUIDE
Top Five Parental Failures

5. RUN, LORI, RUN!

This one's at number five, because of the difficult position Lori found herself in in issue #48. But running into oncoming gunfire with a baby in your arms isn't the best thing to do, is it? Nobody can directly blame her for baby Judith's death and, in a 'normal' situation, when trying to evade gunfire, running is definitely the right choice. But, if you have a baby to look after, your first instinct should be to hide, surely? As dark as this entry is, it has to be considered a fail, because even if Lori had been caught, would the Governor have killed her baby? Maybe. We'll never know.

4. POOR TASTE IN MEN

When we first meet Jessie Anderson, she's married to an abusive sonuvabitch called Pete. As is often the case with abuse victims, she is reluctant to leave him. Thankfully, our main man, Rick, steps in and puts the swine out of his misery. After that, Jessie grows close to Rick who, while having a better moral compass than her ex-husband, is still known for his cutthroat behaviour when it comes to protecting his own. This becomes explicitly apparent when she and Ron follow Mr Grimes and son through a horde of the undead, resulting in their deaths at the teeth of some hungry biters (issue #83). All this happens while she is locked hand-in-hand with Carl. Rick apologizes before chopping her hand off to save his son. Hardcore!

3. SORRY MOM

They say good parenting means making sacrifices. So, giving that extra bottle of wine a miss, or not booking that weekend away at the spa is sometimes a necessity – after all, there's a kid that needs looking after.

It's not all about mom and dad. But poor, tragic Carol clearly had the wrong end of the stick and, while this might be controversial, her efforts to take her own life, on more than one occasion, wouldn't necessarily position her well for Mother Of The Year. Unfortunately for little Sophia, Carol eventually succeeds, when she walks willingly into the embrace of a bloodthirsty zombie, leaving her poor little daughter parentless in issue #41.

2. BAD HAIR DAY

It's a shame to blame old Hershel for this one, but he lost two of his kids in the prison to bloodthirsty killer, Thomas Richards. If you're going to use a prison as your home, you probably shouldn't trust the folk who used to occupy it and let your kiddies run freely about the place. There's no doubt that Richards was chiefly responsible for Rachel and Suzie's gruesome deaths, but Hershel left it a little late to check on their whereabouts, eventually finding them butchered in the prison barber shop. This might be the end of days and walkers may well be the new kings of the food chain, but if there's one lesson that can be taken from *The Walking Dead*, it's that human beings can be pretty evil too. ◇◇◇

1. MAD UNCLE BRIAN

He may only have been her *de facto* dad, but Brian Blake, aka the Governor, made some very bad decisions on behalf of his tragic niece, Penny. She's a walker, for flip's sake; let her die! Instead, he kept her chained up in a cupboard, where he fed her human body parts and even, on occasion, kissed her, which he made possible by removing her teeth. Let's face it, the dude had issues. Hershel may have collected zombies in his barn, but this guy was trying to have some sort of perverse relationship with one. ◇◇

LE OF THE SPECIES

THE PORTRAYAL OF WOMEN IN *THE WALKING DEAD* COMIC

…Is deadlier than the male? Not quite in the case of *The Walking Dead* comic, but the series does depict its female characters in a positive light, portraying them as strong, believable representations of the gender who fight, love and lead on an equal footing to their male counterparts (at least in the latter issues). *TWDM* looks at the evolution of the key female protagonists in the series and explores where the comic gets it right and occasionally wrong…

FEATURE: Lisa Granshaw
BOX OUTS: *TWDM*

A s Rick Grimes struggles to survive the walker apocalypse in Robert Kirkman's *The Walking Dead*, many of the most interesting and compelling characters he meets in his journey are women. Comic books sometimes struggle with their portrayal of female characters in story content and visual depiction. They are often presented as one-dimensional characters or depicted in revealing outfits. The women of *The Walking Dead* manage to escape many of these stereotypes. The majority are fully realized characters that are given the chance to develop – if they survive long enough. The comic, however, is not perfect. In early issues, the depiction of women and their place in society was perhaps less positive. Despite this, the comic has developed to feature some of the best representations of women in the medium today.

SNIPER ELITE

The beginning of the series may have its issues, but it introduces a woman who has continued to survive perhaps better than even Rick: Andrea. It's established fairly quickly once Rick starts to teach Andrea how to use a gun that she is an excellent shot. As the group moves on from the Atlanta camp, Andrea's skills grow and she becomes key to the group's defense and, by proxy, its survival. It takes some time for the others to see her in this way, though, and she has to argue with Rick at several points to let her help clear out walkers, but eventually her skills are acknowledged. By the time the group reaches the prison, there's no question that Andrea will act as the first line of defense as their resident sniper.

Andrea's impressive weapons expertise helps her become a strong, capable character. However, she's not portrayed as a one-dimensional tough woman with a gun. When Andrea has to deal with her sister's death, for instance, she grieves, but does not let it define her. The loss cements the reality of her situation, brings her closer to the older

The comic has developed to feature some of the best representations of women in the medium today.

Dale, and is part of her growth into a character who understands the stakes of the world they're living in. She's shown to be caring and nurturing with her sister (Amy), Dale, and her adopted sons, Billy and Ben. The first time she kills another living person she does not just brush it off. It has an impact on her that she has to accept. Andrea loses many people close to her and it continues to affect her as it would any normal person, but she faces these tragedies and develops as a character because of them.

Andrea's relationships with men are also portrayed as healthy ones. She genuinely loves Dale, and does not immediately need to find another man when he dies. It takes time, but when she ends up with Rick it grows from an unsure relationship to one where they share an intimate connection. Andrea manages to stay true to the tough and

GREENER PASTURES

Another long-time survivor who is allowed to grow over the course of the series in a realistic way is Maggie Greene. She is not given much room to develop as a character before beginning a physical relationship with Glenn, but it never feels like she approached him because she could not be without a man. Instead, the discussion she and Glenn have before sleeping together shows how confident and comfortable with her sexuality Maggie is. Her proposal is more practical from an end-of-the-world view than anything else. When the relationship grows from casual sex into genuine love, it becomes one of the healthiest relationships in the series.

As with Andrea, a lot of Maggie's growth unfortunately results from tragedy. She lost siblings at the farm to walkers, but the senseless deaths of her sisters at the prison led her to shoot and kill their murderer, Thomas Richards. It's a turning point for her character as she begins to work through her depression, face the new reality around her, and accept what she might have to do to survive. When the rest of her family dies, she becomes disheartened and emotional. She relies more on Glenn and even tries suicide. While we may not agree with her decision, her actions are perhaps 'understandable' given the horrors she has faced.

Eventually, Maggie is able to work through her problems and, even after losing her husband Glenn some 40 issues later, becomes a stronger person, for herself, her newborn child, and her adopted daughter, Sophia.

Maggie comes into her own at this point, especially when her leadership abilities begin to take shape at Hilltop. It's no surprise that two years later, after the time-jump, she's firmly in charge and has become a true leader.

compassionate parts of her through all the horror she's seen. The scars on her face are not as disfiguring as Rick's loss of a hand, but they still act as a reminder of all she's been through and survived.

The majority of women in *The Walking Dead* are fully realized characters that are given the chance to develop – if they survive long enough.

MOTHER AND CHILD

The death of Lori and baby Judith in issue 48 of *The Walking Dead* is one of the single most shocking moments in the comic's history. So shocking, in fact, that the storyline was changed for the TV series.

The incident in question takes place during the final stages of the prison assault by the Governor's forces. A hysterical Lori is persuaded by Rick to flee outside, baby in arms, where a prison truck offers a potential means of escape. Their attempted breakout is spotted by the Governor, however, who orders Lilly Caul to stop them at all costs. Lilly fatally shoots Lori in the back, causing her to fall on Judith. As Rick and Carl watch helplessly, the tiny infant is crushed to death under the weight of her mother's body.

A chilling demonstration of the Governor at his most tyrannical, this act proves to be the final nail in his coffin. Lilly turns on him for making her do something so abhorrent, leading to his eventual death.

Despite only appearing in six issues, Lilly is another example of a multifaceted female character within the series. She is obedient only to a point, unlike many of the Governor's male followers. She is genuinely devastated when she finds out she's killed a mother and child and is determined to confront her demons, in this case, the Governor.

Lori's death was changed for the TV series – Lori instead died in childbirth, with baby Judith still very much alive. It's arguable which death is the more horrifying.

Read more about Lilly's story in *The Road To Woodbury, The Fall Of The Governor* and *Descent*.

Many comics too often rely on over-sexualized versions of its female characters... *The Walking Dead* never falls prey to this!

LIVE BY THE SWORD

The most kick-ass female character – and the one that could have easily become a caricature – is Michonne. She was the first female character to be portrayed in a strong, imposing light from the minute she appeared with her katana. From her introduction, it was clear she was a tough, capable, independent woman who could survive on her own. It would have been easy to have her remain just a quiet zombie killer, but luckily that's not all there is to Michonne. She's smart and resourceful, and knows that her best chances of survival are actually with the group. Her independent nature never disappears, but she learns to work with the group, care for them, and becomes essential to their survival.

Michonne is a multi-layered character. Her toughness does not mean she's able to brush off events, as evidenced by the discovery that she's been coping by talking to her dead boyfriend. She admits to worrying about being weak, but learns to open herself up to the others in the group so that she becomes someone whose presence beyond her sword is sorely missed when she's not around – consider how agonizing it has been waiting for her return in the most recent run of the comic.

Michonne's romantic relationships also show that there's more to her than her stony exterior. The men she falls for never define her or change her personality. She truly cares for them and is profoundly affected when she loses both Tyreese and Morgan Jones, but she is still up to the task when it comes to ending their walker-transformed lives. Her budding relationship with Ezekiel too was on her own terms, and only began once she'd seen the vulnerability behind his regal act.

THE RAPE

The rape of Michonne at the hands of the Governor is perhaps the most controversial storyline in the whole series. That it should happen to the strongest woman makes it even more upsetting. The brutality of the attack has been described by some critics as both misogynistic and racist. So was it a justifiable storyline or not?

Firstly, it's a very sad fact that rape happens every day, and is particularly endemic in warzones. To deny that rape would happen under the circumstances seen in *The Walking Dead* would be disingenuous to the truth of this world. Rather than misogynistic, the Governor's attack on Michonne is a true reflection of a terrible and terrifying reality.

So why Michonne in particular? Well, it's definitely about power more than sex. The Governor feels he's already emasculated Rick by removing his shooting hand. But he still feels threatened by this fearsome warrior woman. His leadership is under question, and he wants to mentally break her. That he chooses torture and rape to exact this exemplifies the evil within his egomaniacal make-up.

If the captive had been Carol, for instance, it's hard to imagine the incident ever taking place; indeed, Carol would not have attacked him in the first place. If it was to happen to anyone at all, it almost had to be Michonne. To the Governor, rape is about power, and Michonne is a fierce adversary. In his twisted mind, he sees rape as the only way to control an otherwise indomitable character.

Turning to the accusation of racism, Michonne's skin color did not matter to the Governor. It was about breaking her will power, not about implementing some kind of white supremacy. From a writing point of view, Kirkman had perhaps backed himself into a corner. He made Michonne black to create a strong, positive female character of ethnicity for his comic. When he needed to show the full extent of the Governor's sickness, he had to choose the most powerful woman to inflict it on, and that happened to be Michonne.

Should he have changed the character to a white woman? Would that have diminished the disgust it provokes? Should he have included rape at all? We don't have all the answers, nor would we pretend to, but our opinion is that there's a horrible and horrifying truth to this event that cannot be denied.

At no point are women put in sexy outfits just to sell more issues, or depicted in clothing that makes no sense for their situation.

PICK OF THE REST

Andrea, Maggie and Michonne are the stand-out women characters, but there are other positive portrayals in the comic as well, from younger characters, such as Sophia, to more minor ones.

Alice Warren, for example, is a great female character, even if she didn't last long. A quick learner and calm under pressure, she knows everyone relies on her for medical help, even though she started life as an interior design student. She certainly does not pretend to be a medical expert: she admits when she does not know something and tries to gain as much knowledge as possible in order to help others.

When Lori Grimes is about to give birth, Alice doesn't panic, but handles the situation very well, along with all the other injuries the Governor's attacks on the prison leaves her to combat. She also does not back down from defending the prison, and is one of the only characters interested in discovering what may have caused the walker outbreak.

The other main female characters that play a large role in the comic, Lori and Carol, have more troublesome depictions. Lori toes the line between being sensible and completely panicked. She is very much defined as someone's wife, namely Rick's, more so than any other individual, and remains in that role right up to the point of her death. She often argues with our 'hero,' which almost always paints her as unreasonable and a nag, even though quite often she has a very good point, if only Rick and the others would listen. For instance, it was she who

warned Rick early on not to trust everyone, having acclimatized to the dangers and vagaries of the new world much quicker than her husband. If he had listened sooner, perhaps Rachel and Susie Greene would still be alive today, instead of butchered at the hands of Thomas the serial killer.

Rick's behavior is sometimes deplorable. He often leaves Lori and Carl behind while he goes off on some vital mission, when his place should be with his family. There's no doubt he loves them, and they love him back, but some of his ventures are simply unnecessary. Also, when Lori is pregnant, Rick dismisses her argumentative behavior as the result of hormones, defining her into a sexist stereotype; the overly emotional woman who just cannot help herself.

Perhaps it is because they were a couple before the apocalypse that Rick and Lori are portrayed in this way – the banter between husband and wife that only exists if a relationship has been long-term. Male bravado and sexism is noticeably absent between Rick and Andrea, though. Perhaps he's wary that he'd be shot down faster than a walker at the end of her rifle scope, or perhaps they are both conscious that either of them could be killed at any minute and so they should celebrate each other's worth.

A FRIEND IN NEED

Carol's comic book story arc is realistic up to a point; not everyone would be able to work past these horrific events. Many might become as emotional and unstable as she does. However, her character is almost defined by her mental instability, her flightiness and attachments to others, or lack thereof. Her rapid devotion to Tyreese shows this, as does her attempt to latch on to Rick and Lori when Michonne 'steals' Tyreese.

Carol does demonstrate some strength of character and possibility for change when she voluntarily ends things with Tyreese instead of just putting up with his infidelity. But Carol struggles with both Tyreese and Lori's 'rejection' of her, unable to overcome this even for the sake of her daughter, and as a result just seems overly needy. She never really grows beyond her emotional outbursts, and ultimately attempts suicide not once but twice, finally succeeding in killing herself via zombie bite.

A recent addition to *The Walking Dead* ensemble, Magna, has, however, been well-represented. Again, she's a tough woman, but then to survive in this new world, almost everyone has to be. Magna is almost an amalgam of Andrea, Maggie and Michonne – she's a woman who voices her opinions, has a leadership mentality and a great "bullshit detector," as the comic's editor Sean Mackiewicz recently pointed out in the Letter Hacks section.

Elsewhere, Sophia is steadily gaining a little more

prominence – having previously suffered the minor character malady of only being portrayed with one characteristic (disturbed child). As she hits her teens, alongside the more fleshed out Carl Grimes, it will be interesting to see where Robert Kirkman takes the character as their minds and bodies mature. The addition of a captured teen Whisperer, Lydia, could also provoke some compelling character development in all three.

WHERE THERE'S GOOD THERE'S BAD

It is the larger idea of the woman's role in the post-apocalyptic world that is more problematic than any individual representations. At the beginning of the story, there is a strong sense that the group has easily adopted the idea of men as hunters and women as gatherers. The women are portrayed as doing more menial tasks, often considered a 'woman's job,' such as laundry, sewing, and childcare.

When the outspoken Donna questions why the women are stuck doing the laundry while the men hunt, Lori dismisses her concerns, saying she'd much rather be doing that than facing the dangers associated with hunting. Donna's role is a problematic portrayal: it's great that she brings up women's rights, but her views are too readily rejected. As a result, she appears as an annoying, bad-tempered, nagging wife, complaining about inequality when everything is actually 'fine' according to the others. When Donna finally is given an opportunity to grow, her development is cut short by her death. Until the arrival of Michonne in issue 19, Andrea is the only one who really breaks out of the stereotypical female mold in the early part of the story because she is a great shot, and therefore seen as having 'value.'

Equally, the women seem to be perfectly fine with taking a backseat when it comes to leadership and more often than not are seen to desire the protection of the men. When Rick questions why there are no women on the committee formed at the prison, Dale states that the women said they are OK with the arrangement. To him, it's clear they just want to be protected. It solidifies the idea that women are weaker, in need of protection, and not on the same level as the men in the group. Michonne does take her own initiative on occasions – for instance, when she decides to track down the Governor (notably this ends in disaster however, with her and Tyreese captured, ultimately leading to the latter's murder),

but it's only later, when Maggie takes on the role of Hilltop leader, that a woman is placed solely in charge. Magna too is later seen as the clear leader of the group she brings to the Alexandria Safe-Zone.

THE FEMALE FORM

Luckily, the occasionally shallow portrayal of women never carries over into the art of the comic, even early on. Equally important to how women are portrayed in a story's narrative is how they are visually depicted. Many comics too often rely on over-sexualized versions of its female characters: even though it might not be practical to wear bikini armor or a skintight leotard, women are thrust into an array of revealing outfits that objectify their bodies first and foremost.

The Walking Dead never falls prey to this, instead showing women wearing normal everyday clothes or whatever they can get their hands on, just like the men. What they wear is believable and realistic for their world. At no point are women put in sexy outfits just to sell more issues, or depicted in clothing that makes no sense for their situation. Even when depicting sex and sexual situations in the series, women are never gratuitously exposed.

If there is one complaint of the comic's visual depiction of women it's that they are

The Walking Dead is not a perfect representation of women, but it makes a better effort than many other comics to provide strong, positive representations of the female gender.

more often than not portrayed with very similar body types and levels of attractiveness – certainly the main female characters. Both men and women come in all shapes and sizes, so considering how often the survivors encounter strangers, it would be more realistic if there were at least a little more diversity in the female form (the men are a little more varied in stature).

The Walking Dead is not a perfect representation of women, but it makes a better effort than many other comics to provide strong, positive representations of the female gender. It is also not afraid to change and grow, ditching some of its earlier more negative portrayals for better story and character development for women. •

TOP 5

"I'M THROUGH WITH YOU!"
Top Five Michonne Quotes

ENOUGH'S ENOUGH!

In issue 102, shortly after our heroes' first encounter with Negan, and the harrowing butchery of Glenn in issue 100, Michonne tells Rick she will follow his lead, saying, "I never fought to fight... I fought to live. If you're sitting here telling me you're convinced the move, for now... is to yield, I understand that, because I did see what we're up against. You say I can live by not fighting? I say sure." Until that point, Michonne was always prepared to fight and never cower, so this moment marks a big shift in the power dynamic of the series. ◇◇◇◇◇◇◇◇◇◇

4. SILENCE IS GOLDEN

Michonne's not the best at expressing herself, but her introduction in issue 19 needed nothing more than an ellipsis – just a little "..." Flanked by two toothless zombies on chains, and with her katana in her hand, her arrival into the series is a striking and powerful one. The lack of dialogue actually adds to the impact and, as entrances go, it's a pretty exciting one that sets the tone for her story to unfold. She lets her actions speak louder than her words and is a visual character first, before anything else. Let's face it, as comic book fans, that's what we like. ◇◇◇◇◇◇◇◇◇◇

3. SOMEWHERE TO CALL HOME

Also in issue 19, when Michonne realizes she has an opportunity of safety and to be around people again, she wastes no time in hacking off the heads of the two zombies she had been dragging around to keep her safe, saying, "I won't need them anymore." It gives us an insight into a character who does whatever it takes to survive and to carry on living. This scares and impresses Rick, and the group, all at the same time. But innovation and fearlessness are sought-after qualities when the undead rule the earth, so they're more than glad to have her onboard. Further insight into her ruthlessness comes from learning that the two zombies she kills are actually her former partner and his best friend, Mike and Terry. ◇◇◇◇◇◇◇◇◇◇

FINALLY--I THOUGHT YOU WERE *NEVER* GOING TO WAKE UP.

YOU PASSED OUT A *SECOND* TIME WHEN I NAILED YOUR PRICK TO THE BOARD YOU'RE ON. DO YOU *REMEMBER* THAT? I WOULDN'T DO MUCH *MOVING* IF I WERE YOU.

DON'T WORRY ABOUT THE LITTLE GIRL--I PUT HER IN THE BACK ROOM--WHERE YOU HAD ALL THIS JUNK. WHAT ARE YOU DOING-- BUILDING A *CAGE* FOR YOUR LITTLE--*SEX SLAVE?* WHY DO YOU HAVE HER HERE ANYWAY?

I DON'T EVEN *WANT* TO KNOW.

I'M ANXIOUS TO GET STARTED.

2. EYE FOR AN EYE

After being horrifically raped and beaten by the Governor, Michonne gets her chance for some sweet revenge in issue 39. Now, she's pretty angry, as you can imagine. So, when she gets the bastard alone, she goes to town, telling him, "You passed out a second time when I nailed your prick to the board you're on. Do you remember that? I wouldn't do much moving if I were you." This is about more than punishing the man; she's doing it for womankind and sending a message: it might be the end of days, but you still need to treat women with respect. ◇◇◇◇◇◇◇◇◇◇

1. PUT TO THE SWORD

When Michonne utters an expression like, "I'm through with you," you expect it to precede death and carnage. In issue 71, after seeing flashbacks of her killing zombies and mutilating the Governor, she says it while hanging her sword up on the wall. It's a turning point in her story, and one that marks a change in the mindset of our heroes. For the first time, they feel that they can live again and build a life with one another. Naturally, we know better than that... ◇◇◇◇◇◇◇◇◇

I'M *THROUGH* WITH YOU.

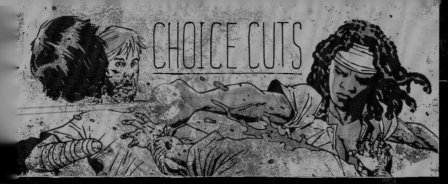
LOVE & ROMANCE

WHEN THE BEATLES WROTE 'ALL YOU NEED IS LOVE,' THEY ALMOST CERTAINLY HADN'T CONSIDERED THE RAMIFICATIONS OF LIVING IN A WORLD POPULATED BY THE UNDEAD, WHERE AN AXE ALSO COMES IN HANDY. HOWEVER, LOVE CAN GROW IN EVEN THE MOST EXTREME SITUATIONS, AND WITH SO MUCH DEATH IN THEIR FACES EVERY DAY, NO ONE CAN BLAME THE SURVIVORS FOR SEEKING SOLACE WITH LOVED ONES, NEW ROMANCES AND OLD FLAMES. WORDS: RICHARD MATTHEWS

TRUE ROMANCE

A lot of the couplings in *The Walking Dead* are born either of lust, power or necessity, but some are genuine expressions of love from people who may never have met otherwise. A prime example is Glenn and Maggie – the longest lasting couple in the comic book and the first to marry within its pages – who may have initially been in it just for the sex, but grew to a deep, profound love that led to marriage and a child. Tragically, Glenn didn't live to see it born.

Other passionate love affairs include teenagers Chris and Julie, who embarked on a tragic suicide pact after consummating their love. Abraham and Holly (who the soldier saved from walker consumption), and Aaron and Eric, who are fiercely protective of each other while working side-by-side as Safe-Zone recruiters.

In AMC's TV show, the great will-they/won't-they romance is Daryl and Carol. The pair have flirted, consoled and supported each other, even though it's been a rocky ride, especially when Sophia was revealed to be a walker. Their romance is yet to be consummated, but the world of *The Walking Dead* is not one to drag your feet in – maybe they're resisting moving beyond friendship because their names rhyme!

"IF YOU'RE ASKING FOR MY APPROVAL YOU'VE GOT IT. KEEP HER HAPPY. KEEP HER SAFE. THAT'S ALL I ASK." HERSHEL, 'THIS SORROWFUL LIFE'

I FOUND YOU, CAROL. EVERYTHING IS PERFECT.

YEAH, IT--QUICK... KNOCK ON WOOD OR SOMETHING.

OH, COME ON.

TOP DOG
RICK

Strength, leadership and the ability to provide food, shelter and safety have come to the fore in society once again, so it's no wonder Rick has had more than one love – Lori, Jessie and Andrea.

And it's nice to see Rick finding kinship with Andrea in the comic. He naturally resisted becoming attached to anyone after losing both his wife Lori and lover Jessie Anderson, convinced that anyone he cares about dies, but theirs appears to be a strong, lasting bond. And God knows – all we want is for Rick to find happiness.

Andrea has, of course, had her own heart broken during the series run. One of the most interesting romances to appear in the comic was her relationship with Dale, which started out as a mere dalliance before developing into a full-blown love affair by the end.

Older man Dale was never fully comfortable in the relationship, believing that Andrea was only with him to stave off loneliness, but he was always glad of the comfort the relationship afforded him. However, no one was left in any doubt that Andrea's love for Dale was anything but real when she bade farewell to him, before firing a bullet through his brain when he turned after being bitten.

"WE SURVIVE THIS BY PULLING TOGETHER, NOT APART."
RICK GRIMES, 'GUTS'

I'LL FUCK YOU.

WHAT?

IF THAT'S WHAT YOU'RE AFTER, I'LL FUCK YOU.

ARE YOU SINGLE?

EXCUSE ME?

LOVE RATS

The apocalypse has really underlined living for the now, being in the present moment. For many, that has meant holding on tightly to their loved ones and never letting go. Inevitably, for others, that meant... well, screwing around.

The most famous in *The Walking Dead* lore is how quickly Shane made a move on Lori. Yes, she's not blameless – whether it's the one-night stand of the comic or the full-blown affair of the show – but it's also fair to say her actions are understandable.

Left alone with Carl, in shock at the wrenching horror around her, assuming Rick is dead, Lori turns to a friend who looks like he can protect them. We don't think Shane's motivations are quite so honorable but, in his defense, he gets a pass for looking after her and Carl during difficult times.

You can't really be as nice about Tyreese and Michonne. Both tough, both alpha personalities – all poor Carol could do was watch (literally) as Michonne took him away from her. Tyreese did pay lip service to

I KNOW WHAT YOU NEED.

Michonne, noting that blowing him was "wrong," but he didn't stop her, and Robert Kirkman's world is one where actions really do speak louder than words. Or grunts. Or moans.

But at least their bond did turn out to be more than just sex, which seems to be a trend among survivors – they may change partners but they generally love harder than they probably did before the outbreak. Look at Abraham and Holly. Gruff ex-soldier Abraham definitely cared for then-partner Rosita, but once he saved Holly's life and they became lovers, you could really see the difference in him. He even talked fondly about Rosita – tragically, just before being killed by a crossbow arrow.

But there are also always sleazes out there: it seemed that no matter how much Regina Monroe stayed loyal to husband Douglas in the Safe-Zone, he still used his position and influence as leader of Alexandria to seduce young women. He even had a crush on Andrea, who was sensible enough not to be remotely interested.

COMFORT BLANKETS

Some bonds are more pragmatic. Circumstance and mutual need are powerful factors in bringing and keeping people together, and for every deeply felt romance, there is one born out of familiarity and shared grief.

In the comic, Carl and Sophia develop a tentative romantic connection based on the lack of anyone else their age around them. It never really progresses beyond affection, however. In the show, they were only friends (and no one will ever forget Sophia's televisual fate – did they feel it would have been too wrenching to end a young romance that way?).

Michonne went after Tyreese for similar reasons – she needed someone as strong as

her, and nothing was going to stop her, let alone Carol.

Elsewhere, a relationship like Dr Denise Cloyd and Heath was a clear sticking plaster on their individual loneliness – Denise had seen Heath at his darkest when Scott died and that brought them together.

But perhaps the bleakest expression of this need for a connection was Carol wanting to have sex one last time before her suicide attempt, going to Billy Greene in his cell. Billy felt used and guilty at the same time after she tried to take her life. But in a zombie-infested world you could die anytime, so what's the odd roll in the sack, really? Or is that just a convenient excuse?

> "I GUESS WE CAN SNUGGLE… IF THAT'S WHAT YOU WANT. YOU BIG GIRL."
> MAGGIE, 'THE HEART'S DESIRE'

> "I WANT HER TO BE HAPPY WITHOUT ME. LIKE I AM WITHOUT HER. I JUST WANT THINGS TO BE RIGHT."
> ABRAHAM, 'SOMETHING TO FEAR'

DOOMED LOVE

Nothing is more romantic than tragedy. Kirkman's creation is not called *The Walking Dead* for nothing, so no one should be surprised that the most consistent end to a romance is the separation of lovers by death.

The story is steeped in grief and melancholy, haunted by literal figures of the past. Some were put out of their romantic misery, others had their last hope ripped cruelly from their grip. Everyone, from major players to the briefest cameos, have been touched by this kind of horror.

Rick and Lori seemed to use up their luck surviving the outbreak then finding each other again. Getting past her indiscretion with Shane used up their last bit of karma, and in both comic book and TV show their marriage ended in Lori's demise.

On the page, Lori was fatally shot in the back during the prison assault, falling and crushing baby Judith in her arms. On TV, she died during a c-section giving birth. This being Kirkman's world, she was then completely eaten by a walker, who Rick discovers with a distended belly containing his deceased wife. Sadly for Rick in the comic, further down the line he also lost lover Jessie when she was killed by walkers before Abraham shot her reanimated corpse.

MAG--!

MAGGIE!

THOKK!

BUT MY FEELINGS FOR HER MEAN I WANT HER TO BE... HAPPY... I DON'T WANT TO BE WITH HER.

I WANT HER TO BE HAPPY WITHOUT ME. LIKE I AM WITHOUT HER. I JUST WANT THINGS TO BE... RIGHT.

DO YOU UNDERSTAND?

IF SHE CAN BE HAPPY WITH YOU... GREAT.

AND THEN...

I JUST DON'T--

As horrible as that was, the horrific moment that probably no fan will ever forget was when Glenn was beaten to death by Negan as retribution for the survivors challenging what he saw as his authority. Glenn whimpered Maggie's name as he died and we all shed a tear (come on – admit it!). Maggie strikes a sad figure from then on, electing to stay at Hilltop with Sophia to fulfill Glenn's final wishes.

The comic book's real Romeo and Juliet moment comes from the deeply sad botched suicide pact between Tyreese's teen daughter Julie and her boyfriend Chris. After making love for the first time, they aim guns at each other and fire. But he shoots too soon (a common complaint with teenage boys, we've heard!), killing her and surviving.

We're then shown there *is* something worse than your child dying in your arms – having your child reanimate in that same embrace. Chris ends her misery just before Tyreese throttles him out of his.

And poor Tyreese was then taken away from Michonne, with The Governor decapitating him with his lover's own katana. Mirroring the fate of his daughter, Tyreese's severed head reanimates and Michonne must finish him off.

> **"WOULDN'T IT BE KINDER TO BE MORE COMPASSIONATE, TO JUST HOLD YOUR LOVED ONES AND WAIT FOR THE CLOCK TO RUN DOWN?" DR EDWIN JENNER, 'TS-19'**

As we consistently discover, in *The Walking Dead* no one is safe. The seemingly unstoppable Abraham had apparently found happiness at last with Holly, only to be killed by one of Dwight's arrows, leaving her devastated and the survivors with a massive hole in their security.

Finally, Hershel Greene took the show to the height of tragedy when it became apparent that his wife Annette had not only become a walker, but that he was keeping her in his barn, hoping desperately for a cure.

Kirkman is a master of making us ask "what would we do?" in some pretty damn nasty

YEAH--I THINK I'M READY.

LET'S DO IT.

OKAY-- NO BACKING DOWN. THIS IS IT.

scenarios, but perhaps the most challenging is "would you be strong enough to 'kill' the ones you love for their own good?"

In all honesty, *TWDM* thinks many of our barns would have necrotizing loved ones scratching at the doors, too.

AAAGH!

BROKEN BONDS

Stressful situations can rip open cracks in relationships and turn them into gaping, irreparable chasms. And there aren't many things more stressful than a walker apocalypse.

There are those, like Tyreese and Carol or basically any relationship The Governor has had on the show, where a new love breaks up an existing couple, or where a break-up is long overdue (did anyone feel sad for Jessie when Rick finally shot her husband and serial abuser Pete?) that you can appreciate why it happened, even in our coddled, intact viewpoint.

Then there's Negan. The leader of the Saviors collects wives like most of us collect pets. The reason he's featured here, rather than anywhere else in this article, is because he takes and destroys at the same time. All you have to do is look at Dwight or Mark's face. Both men burned with an iron because they had the "audacity" to sleep with their wives.

Both Sherry and Amber returned to their respective partners for one night after being married to Negan to basically save their lives and protect their partners, only for Negan to give the men a message they would never forget. In a weird way, the pair of cuckolded survivors are lucky – they could just as easily have ended up shuffling around the Earth like so many other poor souls – but still... •

> "I ALWAYS WANTED TO BE ABLE TO FUCK A WHOLE BUNCH OF WOMEN. SO WHY SETTLE DOWN WITH JUST ONE? I SEE NO REASON TO FOLLOW OLD BORING RULES."
> ### NEGAN, 'WHAT COMES NEXT'

TOP DOG
THE GOVERNOR

In the comic, The Governor doesn't waste time on such things, but in the TV show he had a wife before the outbreak, then had relations with Rowan and Andrea.

CLASH OF THE TITANS

'End Trails' takes a closer look at the best confrontations between characters, as long-time couple Glenn and Maggie are at odds about their future at the Alexandria Safe-Zone…

WORDS: Dan Auty

WHAT'S THE BEEF?

In what turns out to be the last scene we spend with them, Glenn tries to convince Maggie that the group will be safer if they relocate from the Alexandria Safe-Zone to the Hilltop community. With the death of Abraham at the hands of the Saviors still fresh in their minds, Glenn believes that they need a new sanctuary and the Hilltop could provide just that. Maggie, however, needs some convincing to leave the group.

ROUND ONE!

Maggie is quick to put her case forward in the straightforward

manner we've come to expect from her. As she says to Glenn, one fact overrides all others – the Saviors are somewhere beyond the gates of Alexandria and she has no intention of risking another confrontation with them.

ROUND TWO!

Glenn goes for an emotional blow, telling Maggie: "I'm thinking of the baby." Her initial reaction is anger at the presumption that she's *not* thinking of their unborn child. But Glenn is quick to calm her down and explain that he truly believes that this move will be the best thing for them.

THE DECIDING BLOW

Ultimately, Maggie is too tired and too sad to keep up the argument. "I love you and wherever you go I'll follow," she tells him.

AND THE WINNER IS…

Glenn wins this one. By the end of the same issue, they have both hit the road with Rick and Michonne to Hilltop, explaining that they have no intention of returning. But of course, Glenn gets his head caved in by Negan before he even gets that far. Maybe he should've stayed home. •

THE SECRET DIARY OF A WALKER

It's not easy being a zombie in *The Walking Dead* world, as our week in the life/death of an undead walker shows. Diary entries transcribed by Dan Auty…

MONDAY

Dear Diary…

Today is the day I put my suit on, head to school and engage some young minds in the art of learning. Unfortunately, those young minds ended up becoming my lunch on Friday and now I have a messy classroom and a bunch of kids who look even more brainless than usual.

TUESDAY

Staff meeting. Principal Pilato wanted to discuss discipline problems among the 12th grade boys, in particular, this craze of flushing the heads of younger students down the toilet. They keep blocking the pipes and all those headless torsos are

making it almost impossible to open the washroom doors.

WEDNESDAY

Ms Ross, the physical ed mistress, is having trouble running with only one leg, so I had to take her class. It was a disaster – none of the students could manage to go faster than a deathly shuffle. I really wish zombies could run.

THURSDAY

Taking the kids on a trip tomorrow. The last one wasn't a huge success. I misjudged how easily an undead body can come apart on a rollercoaster. I was apologizing to the principal for showering him in offal for days.

FRIDAY

We all went to the local prison. Big mistake! For a start, it didn't seem very safe – the gates were wide open! Then this bunch of normos turned up with trucks and swords and started causing trouble. I barely made it out of there intact – lost a few of my class along the way, but they were never going to amount to much anyway. What a week?! •

TOP 5

SMILEY FACE
Five Moments of True Joy

5. IRON FIST

Carl Grimes has not had much joy in his life, after all he's been shot (twice), almost raped and lost his mother and baby sister, so any moments of happiness for him should be richly cherished. When his father agrees to let him become apprentice to the Hilltop's blacksmith, Earl, in issue 128 it's a real fist-pump moment for the young man. His disappointment at finding out Earl already has an apprentice is quickly dissipated when the blacksmith points out there's no reason why he can't have two apprentices. Yay – go Carl! ◇◇◇◇◇◇◇◇

4. SHOTGUN WEDDING

There's no such thing as wedding planning during an apocalypse, that's for sure. That doesn't stop Maggie and Glenn getting hitched though. Their choice of venue isn't the best – the prison cafeteria – but, options are limited, after all.

The main thing is that the father of the bride, Hershel, is overjoyed. Also, everyone they love is in attendance while they say their vows to one another. That should suffice, eh? What more do you need?

3. BOOKWORMS

They say knowledge is power. If that is the case, in a time where power is everything, finding the prison library in issue 20 is a big win for our gang of hardy inmates. Sure, books won't fix all their problems, but they, like everyone else, need some escape from time to time. Having literature certainly helps bring that to them; being trapped behind gates and barbed wire fences 24 hours a day – although safer than being out in the wild where they're hunted by the undead – isn't always good for the mind. The library also helps bring a little normality to life behind bars, with Hershel even starting a garden. ◇◇◇◇◇◇◇◇◇◇◇◇◇◇◇◇◇◇◇◇

2. NEW LIFE

Newborn babies bring added complications, we all know that. It's a given. Nevertheless, with death so abundant in *The Walking Dead*, new life can only be a welcome thing. Baby Judith's arrival in issue 39 is a moment that reduces our hard-knock heroes to blubbering, jibber-jabbering buffoons and, you know what, they need it. Maternal and paternal instincts abound after her birth, bringing new purpose to the group: creating a better life for the future. Her birth represents hope and an acceptance that mere survival just won't do. ◇◇◇◇◇◇◇◇◇◇◇◇

1. OLD FRIENDS

There are several key reunion moments during *The Walking Dead* but, after some pretty dark times on the road, Rick and Carl's reunion with Michonne in issue 52 is pretty timely and one that ends in a big hug for little Carl. Taking on the apocalypse alone can be testing and when Papa Grimes leaves to scavenge for some gas, young Carl is attacked by a walker. Thankfully, our katana-wielding friend steps in to save the day. Phew! Some reunions are all hugs and smooches, but this one is so much more. A real life-saver. ◇◇◇◇◇◇◇◇◇◇◇◇◇

A LARGER WORLD

IN A NUTSHELL

TITLE: A Larger World
FEATURED ISSUES: 91-96
COLLECTION: Volume 16
SYNOPSIS: Rick and the members of the Alexandria Safe-Zone discover they are not the only large group of survivors when a scout for another town, the Hilltop Colony, introduces himself, asking to open up trade routes between the two. Rick realizes that Alexandria has little to offer the peaceful Hilltop community, until he learns that they are under constant threat from a large, aggressive group called The Saviors, led by the mysterious Negan. Rick offers to protect the colony from them in exchange for food rations and other necessities.
TIDBITS:

- It's revealed that it's been nearly two years since the zombie outbreak began.
- There are at least 200 people living at the Hilltop Community.
- There are several hints that Rick and Andrea are forming a bond that goes beyond friendship.
- Although mentioned several times, Savior leader, Negan, does not appear in this story arc at all. He makes his first dramatic entrance in issue 100.

Over the course of its run, *The Walking Dead* has featured some enthralling storylines, but what is it about them that make them so captivating? In 'Anatomy Of A Story', we dissect Robert Kirkman's ideas into their component parts, analyze them in-depth and offer our conclusions on what make them tick. With 'Something To Fear' (see page 100) providing a good stepping on point for fans new to the comic, **Stuart Barr** employs his scalpel for a closer examination of the immediately preceding tale, *'A Larger World.'*

The 100th issue of any comic is a milestone, but it is especially impressive for a series that has been as consistently bleak and challenging as Robert Kirkman's *The Walking Dead*. There has been such a glut of zombie films, novels and comic books since the debut issue of the series that it is easy to forget that when issue one hit the shops back in 2003, the Noughties' zombie renaissance had yet to really shamble into view (or in the case of Zach Snyder's remake of *Dawn Of The Dead*, sprint off the starting line like Usain Bolt).

By 2004, zombies were back, baby, with both the *DOTD* remake and Edgar Wright and Simon Pegg's *Shaun Of The Dead* released. In 2003, *The Walking Dead* must have seemed like a risky proposition.

For the majority of the comic's run, the story has focused on former police officer Rick Grimes, his immediate family and the survivors that gather around him. Apart from their extended stay in the prison, the group has been on the run, never settling down for long before being forced to uproot again to flee the zombie menace. Things changed with issue 70, when Rick

WE'RE HERE.

WELCOME TO THE HILLTOP.

AAGH

Rick's focus on protecting Carl at the expense of all others has consistently taken them into harm's way.

and his group were taken to the Alexandria Safe-Zone, a walled-in community living a semblance of a normal suburban existence. There have been dramas, but over the time we have spent with Rick and the other survivors in Alexandria they have found something potent, something they had forgotten in the desperate struggle for survival.

The group has been fighting for their lives, conflict has been rife, and Rick has been physically and psychologically crippled. He has dealt with the physical, but the psychological damage has been far more severe. Fixated upon keeping his son, Carl, safe at all costs, Rick gave up on his role as leader, putting his son's interests, and then his own before that of the group.

Among the survivors, no one has properly risen to become a uniting leader; all of them have pulled in different directions during Rick's abdication of the role. What they all begin to rediscover in Alexandria is the concept of 'community', and the safety and comfort of being part of something larger than the self. This theme takes center-stage in *A Larger World*.

The story arc begins a few weeks after the dramatic siege

of Alexandria by the undead that cost many lives and left Carl in a coma. Rick has come to realize that his focus on protecting Carl at the expense of others, rather than keeping them all safe, has actually taken them into harm's way. Had he trusted in the safety garnered from numbers, his son would not have been maimed by a stray bullet, and he wouldn't have had to sacrifice the lives of several others.

Rick resolves to change, again stepping up to the challenge of leadership. As he's proved on countless occasions, he's at his best in a crisis, and Alexandria is about to face several.

When Carl awakes he is suffering from amnesia due to his head trauma, leading to a heartbreaking moment when Rick must again explain that his mother has gone. Carl actually takes the news with grim determination. His father had hopes that the relative safety of Alexandria would allow Carl to become a child again, but it's clear that the horrors the boy has endured has now made that a pipe dream.

The loss of childhood and the effect of this grim new world on children is one of the themes that Kirkman has been

OPPOSITE PAGE: Hilltop seems to be perfect, and Rick knows opening a trade route would solve a lot of problems. ABOVE: Can 'Jesus' be trusted? TOP RIGHT: Carl must face his own demons.

developing in the book over the last few volumes. At the same time, children are resilient and find their own mechanisms of coping; for instance, Sophia tells Carl that she knows her parents are dead, but it makes her happy to pretend that Glenn and Maggie are her mom and dad. Still, one can't help but feel there will be issues for Carl further down the road.

Another problem is that Alexandria's food supplies are running out and winter is on the horizon. The survivors pull together, first sending a small party to thoroughly explore the area around Alexandria before moving further afield in the search for food and supplies. The pickings are lean, but this is expected.

Matters take a surprising turn when a stranger who has been observing the community makes his presence known. Paul Monroe, aka Jesus, claims to be an envoy from another larger community called Hilltop. He astonishes Rick by claiming that there are several other communities in the Washington area, and that trade routes are established. Paul wants to open a new route between the Hilltop and Alexandria colonies, but Rick and those closest to him have learnt to be suspicious.

Is there anything to be taken from Paul's nickname 'Jesus'? Paul claims it is due to his long hair and beard, but he also has the look of a zealot about him. Rick interprets this as proof of guilt, telling Andrea that his confidence, restraint and lack of fear while being held captive is a bad sign, noting, "The guilty man sleeps in his cell while the innocent one climbs the walls with worry."

This is partly Rick's experience as a police officer coming to the fore, but it is also the wrong call. It may be that Paul is unafraid because he has belief, belief that Hilltop and the fledgling federation of small communities around it are the future for humanity. Paul is also shown as a man of action and a skilled warrior, and yet despite being openly threatened, he refuses to attack Rick or his associates, only defending himself. Whether there is more to his nickname will perhaps become apparent in the future.

Eventually, Paul takes Rick and a small group to Hilltop where they discover he *has* been telling the truth. Suddenly, there is a world outside of Rick's immediate

Hilltop has accepted the death of the pre-apocalypse world. Theirs is a brave new world, and one that cannot afford to be insular.

OPPOSITE PAGE, CLOCKWISE FROM FAR LEFT: Jesus is forced to overcome a fractious reaction from Rick and his group; but Rick realizes he needs to be less insular, both on the personal level of his relationships, and by acknowledging the bigger post-apocalyptic picture.

THIS PAGE, LEFT: Rick makes a bargain with the Hilltop community which he will live to regret ABOVE: Rick has also lost trust in everyone other than his closest family and friends. BELOW: The world will never be the same again, and neither will *The Walking Dead*.

group. Suddenly, there is concrete evidence of a new society that is self-sufficient, sustainable and isn't holding out for rescue, evacuation or vaccines. They have accepted that the restoration of the old pre-apocalypse world is a fantasy. This is a brave new world, and one that's no longer so insular.

Of course, this is *The Walking Dead* and nothing is ever that simple. All the best zombie stories share one thing: this may sound counter-intuitive, but they aren't about zombies. The best stories of this type are about the survivors, and the villains are

not zombies, they are other survivors. These connected communities are like a herd of wildebeest, grouping together for strength and safety.

But where there are herds, there are predators. In this case, a bandit group called The Saviors who are surviving by forcing Hilltop to give them 50 per cent of their produce or face a campaign of terror. Even before this revelation, Rick has realized that Alexandria has little to offer in a barter system – they don't grow crops and their

stocks of food and medicine are low.

However, he sees an opportunity: the group of survivors he's led across the barren North American landscape are essentially battle-hardened veterans. Rick

offers Hilltop his services in fighting off The Saviors. Despite dissenters within his group, including the normally supportive Michonne, Rick sees this as an opportunity to, in his words, "finally stop surviving, and start living". •

PAUL 'JESUS' MONROE

With his introduction into the TV series, *TWDM* thought it was time to look at the character of Paul Monroe, aka Jesus, in our character spotlight section. In a nutshell, he's as badass as they come. WORDS: Dan Auty

FIRST APPEARANCE

Jesus is first introduced as a mysterious figure at the start of issue 92, observing the residents of Alexandria at a distance with a pair of binoculars in one hand and a gun in the other. By this point in the comic, it's not unreasonable to expect that any new characters – especially those who are seen sneaking around at night, spying on our heroes – might be hostile.

A few pages later we find out a little more, but his intentions are still unclear. Emerging from behind a car, shortly after Michonne and Abraham have dispatched a group of walkers, Jesus is immediately held at knifepoint by Michonne. But Jesus quickly reverses the situation, disarming her and holding the same blade to her throat. Throughout this confrontation, we hear a calm, polite voice of reason that soon becomes one of Jesus' defining characteristics.

"Honestly, I really just want to talk," he tells her. "Is there someone slightly more calm who I could possibly have a discussion with?"

FIGHT NIGHT

The speed at which Jesus disarms Michonne is impressive during their first encounter, but it is really only a taster for his first true display of his fighting skills, which happens a couple of issues later. Having been taken prisoner by Rick and the others, they stop their van for the night on the way to the Hilltop, where they plan to meet Jesus's associates. The discovery that Carl is stowed away next to Jesus is quickly forgotten when a group of walkers suddenly appear. Jesus leaps from the van and, with his arms still tied behind his back, manages to deflect several zombies using just his feet, spinning and pivoting in a spectacular display of 'kung-foot' work.

As Rick says: "That was impressive."

Jesus's response is typically modest: "Just trying to do my part."

A later encounter with Negan in issue 114 produces similar results; it takes Jesus only seconds to remove Negan's bat from his grasp and put a gun to his head. "Why the fuck hasn't someone shot you?" a furious Negan demands. "Your soldiers suck!" comes the nonchalant reply.

WORST/BEST MOMENT

Fact is, Jesus is braver and smarter than most of his enemies. This doesn't mean that he doesn't ever get captured – and this being *The Walking Dead*, he'll probably end up dead sooner or later. But he keeps fighting, and always looks for the way out of a tight spot.

In issue 104, Jesus has been dispatched by Rick to trail Dwight back to Negan's base to find out its location, and how big his army is. He is spotted and finds himself outnumbered by a group of Saviors, but despite the odds, he nearly overcomes his enemies with a flurry of feet and hands. Being captured, tied up, and bundled into the back of a jeep is no real obstacle either; within a few pages, Jesus is free of his ties and has rolled off the back of the vehicle unnoticed. But not before he's discovered exactly where Negan's headquarters are, information of vital importance to Rick for the upcoming war.

KILLER LINE

While Jesus remains an enigmatic figure, there is no doubt that he inspires the friendship, trust, and loyalty of many of the people whom he encounters. One of the most important introductions he makes for Rick and his group is to Ezekiel. The Kingdom is part of what Jesus describes as "the network" of allies and associated groups, and Jesus has made sure that Hilltop has forged close links with Ezekiel's group of armored, sword-wielding 'knights.' As eccentric as King Ezekiel is, he is clearly close to Jesus, allowing him to ride freely into his lands and greeting him with a warm welcome: "It pleases me to see you, old friend."

One of our favorite lines in the whole of *The Walking Dead* series also happens at this point, as Jesus explains to a shocked Rick: "Oh, I think I forgot to mention… Ezekiel has a tiger." The look on Rick's face at the sight of Shiva is priceless and we can't help but think Jesus delayed giving him that particular piece of information just to see Rick's jaw drop, the cheeky chap. It seems we're not the only ones who love this moment and line either, as it made it onto its own Skybound T-shirt.

JESUS THE DISCIPLE

All of Jesus' positive attributes – his physical and fighting skills, his bravery and intuition, his cool head and loyalty – would suggest that he would make a natural leader. But it seems he prefers to follow, to help those in command achieve what they want. This could be because he lacks that one key element that someone such as Rick has – a ruthless streak, that leads him to take unpopular, sometimes brutal, decisions in order to protect the wider group.

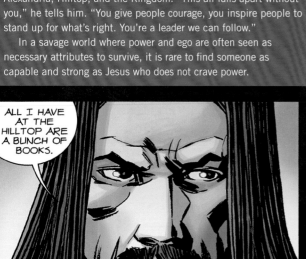

Jesus also knows that Ezekiel doesn't have this: despite his hatred of Negan, Jesus only chose to do something about him once Rick was on the scene. In issue 114, Jesus tells Rick why he must lead the collected people of Alexandria, Hilltop, and the Kingdom. "This all falls apart without you," he tells him. "You give people courage, you inspire people to stand up for what's right. You're a leader we can follow."

In a savage world where power and ego are often seen as necessary attributes to survive, it is rare to find someone as capable and strong as Jesus who does not crave power.

BOOK WORM

The loyalty that Jesus has to those he believes in is shown to its full extent in issue 116. Rick has led a large group from the three communities – Alexandria, Hilltop, and the Kingdom – to the gates of the Saviors' compound, to tell Negan that they will no longer "negotiate" with him, or provide him with a regular share of their supplies. Negan brings Gregory out, who announces that Hilltop will remain with the Saviors, and unless the Hilltop residents among the group immediately head home, they and their families will be cast out into the wilderness. Rick understands Jesus's position – he has been a member of the Hilltop for a long time. "I'll understand," he tells him. Jesus's response, however, is a classic mix of defiance and loyalty, mixed with a melancholy at his loner status: "All I have at the Hilltop are a bunch of books."

THE LOOK

Jesus is one of the most distinctive characters in the series. Pre time-jump (issue 126), Jesus is a mix of rock dude and hobo, with his long hair, fuzzy beard, and trademark long coat, snood, and beanie combo. The beard and hair are almost certainly where his nickname came from – he doesn't appear overly religious, for instance.

Post time-jump, Jesus is still rocking the beard and long hair, but is now styled more like an ancient samurai, with a top knot reminiscent of the warrior race. It's a look reinforced by his new body armor and sword. All he needs now is one of those cool-looking helmets...

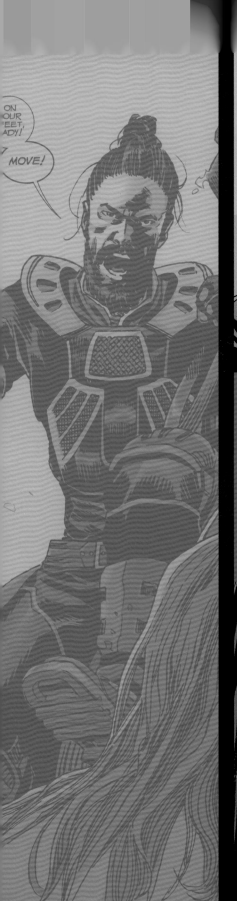

RELATIONSHIPS

So Jesus may not be the first openly gay character to appear in *The Walking Dead*, but he's the coolest, in our humble opinion. His sexuality is dealt with matter of factly, as it is with every other character. Creator Robert Kirkman once wrote: "In my opinion, there should be more awesome gay people in fiction because there are plenty of awesome gay people in real life. I want Jesus to be a character where his sexuality is as unimportant as Rick or other heterosexual characters. So we won't focus on it constantly and it won't be the focus of any big storylines for him... but he'll make out with a dude every now and then... before going out and drop-kicking zombies. He's one of my current favorite characters."

FLAWED HERO

In case it is starting to sound like Jesus is some kind of all-knowing, kung fu-kicking saint, he is definitely not without his flaws. He makes a potentially crucial mistake in issue 109, which comes as a direct result of his trusting nature. Rick asks him to go around the different communities and get their support for a combined assault on Negan.

One of those he speaks to is his Hilltop neighbor, Kal. He asks Kal to estimate how many men Hilltop can provide for the attack, without leaving the community unprotected. However, Kal's subsequent disappearance makes Jesus realize he's going to Negan with the information, and they are about to be betrayed by someone he considered a friend. "How could I be so stupid?" he laments.

Kal's actions come from a place of fear of the consequences rather than any loyalty to Negan, but Jesus's mistake is in believing that everyone sees the situation the same way he does.

RAY OF SUNSHINE

Once the time-jump has occurred, we see that Jesus has settled into the role of scout and soldier. He chooses to stay in Alexandria rather than return to the Hilltop, and splits his time between keeping zombie herds away from the residents and finding new survivors to bring into the community. The encounter with the Whisperers presents the group with the first real human threat since the Saviors were defeated, and presents Jesus with a vital role.

When Lydia is captured, Jesus takes on the role of trying to extract information from her. It is via his calm, focused interrogation that we learn the first pieces of information about this new enemy: why they wear masks of flesh, their attitudes toward innocence and childhood, and their general philosophy about how the dead have rightfully inherited the world from the living. Jesus even has time for a little joke, replying to Lydia's doom-laden mantra with, "Aren't you a ray of sunshine?"

> AREN'T YOU A RAY OF SUNSHINE?

JESUS THE SAVIOR

The relative safety of the community at this stage doesn't preclude Jesus from indulging in a bit of old-school martial arts action. When Gregory decides to take back Hilltop from Maggie, he gives her a glass of poisoned wine. But he doesn't count on Jesus coming into his house at the exact moment that Maggie collapses to the ground. Flying across the room, feet first, he knocks Gregory into the wall and rushes to help Maggie. Gregory splutters his innocence, but Jesus simply tells him, "You're a fucking dead man." Maggie comes to and defuses the situation, instead throwing Gregory into a cell. Jesus might be a calm, wise, level-headed man, but this scene is a nice reminder that when it comes down to it, his feet can do all the talking. •

MAKING A SPLASH!

One of the highlights of Charlie Adlard's *The Walking Dead* artwork is his tremendous splash panels (full page or double page illustrations). They are used relatively minimally, but when done, they are always memorable. *TWDM* looks at some of the most impactful splashes to feature in the comic. **WORDS: Dan Auty**

HOW DID WE GET HERE?

This splash appears early on in issue 95. New character Paul has led Rick, Michonne and three others from their group to the outer walls of the Hilltop community. Rick explains his reluctance to take his people into the stronghold, fearing that they will be hugely outnumbered; Paul assures Rick that they can keep their weapons. But just as they approach the gates, a shambling walker steps into their path.

WHAT'S THE SCENE?

A wide vista, the long, high walls of the Hilltop community stretching the full width of the panel in the background. In the foreground, Glenn, Andrea, Carl, Rick and Paul watch as Michonne deals with the unfortunate zombie.

SILENCE IS GOLDEN

The impact of the artwork, freed from the confines of individual panels, is of course the huge advantage of a splash panel. Which isn't to say that Robert Kirkman and Charlie Adlard don't often use splashes to highlight dramatic points with key uses of dialogue, but cases such as this one demonstrate that sometimes a single drawing can say as much as a dozen speech bubbles.

PICTURE PERFECT

With an illustration like this, Adlard proves he's as much a master of the epic widescreen image as he is with intense, claustrophobic close-ups. The driving rain adds a tremendous amount of atmosphere, as does the dramatic darkening sky. The silhouetted figures on the walls suggest the mystery and potential danger that lies beyond, while the relaxed, almost casual manner with which our heroes stand while Michonne lops the walker's head off shows just how accustomed they are to such sights. It's a beautiful illustration that reveals any number of details about the characters and their situation. •

THE SECRET DIARY OF A WALKER

It's not easy being a zombie in *The Walking Dead* world, as our week in the life/death of an undead walker shows. Diary entries transcribed by Dan Auty…

MONDAY

Dear Diary…

The last thing I remember was going to get a haircut at Zeb's Ironic Disco Salon. There was some commotion when a guy wouldn't pay for his beard trim, and he took a bite out of the DJ that Zeb pays to play dubstep for customers. Next thing I know I'm waking up amid piles of hair, half-eaten limbs and blood-splattered skateboard magazines.

TUESDAY

Stopped by my girlfriend Amber's apartment to play *Cosmic Encounter* and pick up my Frightened Rabbit 7-inch I'd lent her. She wasn't home, but I did some gaming anyway. Unfortunately, my rotting thumbs kept slipping off the controller, and the view of the TV was somewhat obscured by brain matter on the screen.

WEDNESDAY

Finally caught up with Denny. He's been lying low – mostly because his legs have been severed at the knees. He reckoned Amber had headed to the countryside to look for food. Couldn't really take him with me, so I left him with my iPad and told him to FaceTime me if he found any fresh organs to chow down on.

THURSDAY

Got to this farm and found Amber. Had made sure my hair had the perfect side parting and was wearing my best specs and favorite Tee, but she hardly noticed cos she was feasting on some country hicks. Great news though, we discovered that the kid who lived here was way into their downtempo electronica. We decided to hang out in the country for a while – ironically, of course.

FRIDAY

Not a good day. Discovered a huge collection of Coldplay albums in one of the other rooms, so we tried to warn the neighboring normos about this terrible discovery. Didn't go so well – Amber kept falling over and I was so distraught, I kept fumbling my words. Then one of the normos stuck a knife through my brain. Squares! •

TWDM'S Guide To The Kingdom

The Walking Dead Magazine takes an in-depth look at the Kingdom, yet another survivor group that was introduced in season six of the AMC show and plays a big part in season seven...
WORDS: Russell Cook

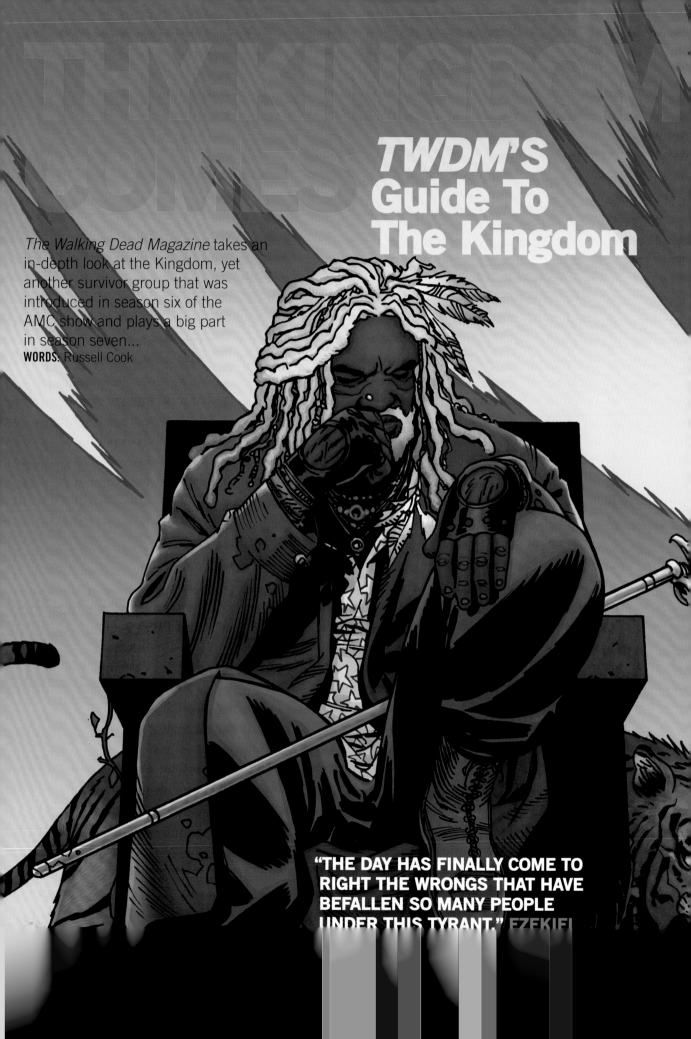

"THE DAY HAS FINALLY COME TO RIGHT THE WRONGS THAT HAVE BEFALLEN SO MANY PEOPLE UNDER THIS TYRANT." EZEKIEL

Negan finally arrived on our screens in season six, and, let's face it, having made his introduction by beating one of our heroes to a pulp, times seemed pretty bleak. But, despite the coming of such dark days, Rick and the gang weren't as alone as they thought, with the season finale introducing another new group.

For comic book readers, these new folk were familiar. The way they looked, and the empathetic and humane manner in which they treated Morgan and Carol, suggested they were from the Kingdom – a community that is the antithesis to the Saviors' reign of terror and oppression. The self-proclaimed King of the Kingdom, Ezekiel, leads his people with a softer touch than his counterpart at the Sanctuary, making the Kingdom an ideal ally for the Alexandria and Hilltop communities.

BACK TO SCHOOL

The Kingdom is first introduced in issue 108 of the comic series, when Jesus – one of the main figures at the Hilltop – takes Rick to meet its leader, Ezekiel. The place is an old, abandoned school in Washington DC and is occupied by, you guessed it, a group of survivors. It has its own rules and hierarchy, quite different to any of the other safe-zones. And, most importantly, its leader seems like a reasonable guy with a legitimate distaste for the Saviors.

Surrounded by buses and large sheets of metal for added fortification, the Kingdom is structurally sound and, over time, does a good job of keeping out the undead. Its survivors spend the summer months camping in tents outside, which is testament to how safe they feel living there. But that hasn't stopped the malevolence of the living from infiltrating their perceived feeling of safety, as the community is one of several

"THE KINGDOM IS THE BIGGEST SETTLEMENT WE KNOW OF OUTSIDE OF THE HILLTOP." JESUS

that has a 'deal' with Negan, giving up half of its supplies whenever demanded.

As plans for bringing Negan down are devised, in issues 108 to 114, we are given a little bit more of an insight into the Kingdom. Its people appear to share the values of Alexandria and the Hilltop: they want to survive and are trying

to rebuild a life, by establishing a community with a future. In issue 111, despite Michonne and Ezekiel drawing swords on one another when they first meet – just a misunderstanding after he tried to kiss her hand (early indication of a frisson between the two) – our heroes are treated to a feast in the school's cafeteria. It's a civilized affair that represents the community's push towards further civility.

STRUCTURAL INTEGRITY

Ezekiel's Kingdom is a unique place. With a school at its core, the iconography of it is a powerful visual reminder of the world before the apocalypse. The yellow buses that form a wall around it, along with the Stars and Stripes flag that flies at full mast above, recall a lost period that serves as aspiration for a return to normality. Its leader is also a wise-cracking old man, with a pet tiger (you will read more about that shortly). His subjects respect him – something he has earned not through fear or intimidation, but by positive presence and personality.

Security guards ride around on horses and are covered in homemade body armor. When you think about it, that's quite a step forward from the chaotic and unruly way the rest of the world seems to fight its battles now that the dead roam the Earth. Another unique quirk of its people is that they camp during the summer. Most of us won't camp in a nearby park for fear of catching up with the local freak in the middle of the night, but this lot do it during the zombie apocalypse.

Perhaps most interesting, though, is how the Kingdom's people extend a hand to others who need help. Even our heroes, Rick and his Atlanta survivor group, have happily fed off the weak when it justified their own needs, but Ezekiel and his men seem more humane and less self-motivated.

ALL THE KING'S MEN

The Kingdom's biggest personality is Ezekiel. As its self-proclaimed king, he projects a confident and knowledgeable persona. However, it's sometimes perceived as arrogance. He's an older man, with long white dreadlocks and a cheeky but charming personality, which has the potential to get him into more scrapes, like the one mentioned earlier with Michonne. But that charisma is also what endears him to people.

As his name suggests, Ezekiel exudes wisdom – in biblical terms, Ezekiel was a prophet of God and has his own book in the Hebrew Bible. Instead of trying to fight the Saviors as soon as Negan shows up, he's patient. He knows that it will take planning and a real army to defeat the enemy, so he waits. It's only when Rick Grimes turns up on his doorstep that he knows the time is right. It's this sort of good judgment that inspires the people of the Kingdom.

However, what they don't know is that there is a deeply insecure part of Ezekiel's personality hidden away, which we find out later on in the story.

He's also clearly quite eccentric. Probably the most visually striking thing about Ezekiel is the pet tiger at his side. Her name is Shiva and,

while that is pretty awesome, it does make him seem a little mad. But hey, it's not a quality to be sniffed at in a world where perception is everything.

That eccentricity is, in part, what allows him to retain an air of otherness and being a cut above the rest. His syntax, his presentation, his throne, his knights on horseback, his loyal (and terrifying) pet – all of these things suggest Ezekiel is a born leader, both kingly and wise.

But, as we soon find out, Ezekiel is actually of a much more humble origin: in a quiet moment, he reveals to Michonne that pre-apocalypse he was merely a zookeeper and has known Shiva since her birth. The two formed a fast bond and have survived the rising of the undead together, despite her having attacked him in the past. Nowadays, she remains calm and non-confrontational, unless encouraged by her master. His 'royalty,' he reveals comes from a history of amateur dramatics: "I used to act in community theater. The King Ezekiel bit comes as second nature to me."

Richard is the other key character from the Kingdom, or at least the only other one who plays any integral role in the comic series. He introduces himself as the Kingdom's head of security in issue 115 and, logically, is Ezekiel's second-in-command. He's seen becoming involved in the planning of the attack on the Saviors and the Sanctuary and, while we don't get to know him too well in the comic, his presence is an important part of the show.

"DINE. ENJOY THE BOAR WE'VE SLAUGHTERED IN YOUR HONOR. EAT AND BE MERRY! FOR TOMORROW WE GO TO WAR!" EZEKIEL

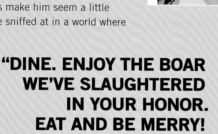

REVENGE IS A DISH BEST SERVED COLD

From the moment Rick tells Ezekiel of his plan to attack the Saviors, the value of the King's calm head cannot be underestimated. His apparent wisdom, and ability to inspire his own people, means that Rick has a useful, trustworthy, and powerful ally.

The Kingdom is key in the build-up to 'All Out War' in issue 115, serving as a base for planning their approach – like a war room, of sorts. And when the battle begins, Ezekiel and his people are right in the thick of the fight.

It's obvious from the very first skirmish, at the gates of the Sanctuary, that the Kingdom's involvement in the war is vital to a successful outcome. During the fight, Ezekiel is charged with guiding the allies to take out the Saviors' snipers, who are picking their troops off one-by-one. He does it with aplomb, before shepherding everyone onto buses and to safety, as a zombie horde is drawn to the chaos – all part of the plan.

Ezekiel later orders his people to abandon the Kingdom. He wants them to be with Rick's people at the Hilltop, closer to the fight with ▶

83

"PEOPLE WANT SOMEONE TO FOLLOW. MAKES THEM FEEL SAFE. PEOPLE WHO FEEL SAFE ARE MORE USEFUL. LESS DANGEROUS... MORE PRODUCTIVE."
EZEKIEL

Negan. He believes that being by Rick's side is the only way to survive and knows that strength in numbers is everything.

It's here that his relationship with Michonne blossoms and we learn of his own insecurities as a leader, and the guilt he feels for losing his warriors and the things he loves most during the fighting. But, with the support of Michonne, he picks himself up and soldiers on, side-by-side, with everyone else until the Saviors are eventually defeated.

"I WAS ARROGANT. I WAS ALSO FOOLISH. IT TOOK ME FAR TOO LONG TO REALIZE THIS BATTLE WAS OVER... THAT WE'D LOST."
EZEKIEL

WHEN ALL'S SAID AND DONE

We don't hear an awful lot about the Kingdom after the war, at least not until Issue 139, when Rick and Ezekiel meet at the coast.

Following the two-year time jump, we learn that Michonne, who we'd assumed was at the Kingdom, has

WERE DUE YESTERDAY. OULD ROLL ANY TIME NOW.

IT'S DEFINITELY NOT THE WORST PLACE IN THE WORLD TO WAIT.

"I CAN FIGHT. I HAVE TO FIGHT. MY PEOPLE DEPEND ON ME. AND I DON'T WANT ANYONE ELSE TO SUFFER THE KIND OF LOSS I HAVE."

EZEKIEL

been away at sea for quite some time on a scouting mission, suggesting her relationship with the King is no more. On a more positive note, it seems that the Kingdom is officially back up-and-running and has a trade deal established with Alexandria and the Hilltop.

That rosy news doesn't last long though. In issue 144, Rick finds Ezekiel's head impaled on a spike, along with several other victims. It seems there's a new threat on the horizon: a group known as the Whisperers. Its leader, Alpha, kills Ezekiel and numerous others, making her group's presence known with a bang. It is perhaps an ignoble end to the character, but given his 'royalty' perhaps it's also fitting – leaving decapitated heads on spikes as a warning has its roots historically with rulers dating back centuries.

This fatalistic act once again changes the course for the Kingdom, leaving it leaderless. In issue 151, Rick suggests Michonne take the reins and fill the void, but any plans to establish order are quickly quelled when Negan, who has been in prison for several years, since the end of 'All Out War,' escapes. It seems the Kingdom might just need to get ready to do battle once more and leadership is needed now more than ever. •

KING EZEKIEL

Since his arrival in issue 108, when he even got his own cover, King Ezekiel has become one of the more compelling new(-ish) characters in the comic book series. Here we present his key moments, words and actions to date.

WORDS: Rich Matthews

HIS FIRST APPEARANCE

The cover of issue 108 tells you everything you need to know – Ezekiel, eyes lowered, white dreads hanging regally around his shoulders, laconically sits on a throne, his scepter in hand and – most strikingly – a tiger lurks behind him making eye contact with the reader. It's a striking image, second only to Michonne's introduction in terms of its impact. A lot of the image's power undeniably comes from Shiva, Ezekiel's 'pet' tiger – a totem of strength, power and command if ever there was one. The tiger is even named after the Hindu god of destruction.

It's the ever-present threat Shiva represents that allows Ezekiel to strike such a benevolent, even charming pose while maintaining authority as he rules over The Kingdom. He's an ambiguous character in this issue – seemingly benign towards Rick and the other survivors, but potentially also a little crazy and perhaps not the most trustworthy of allies. But, as the saying goes, the enemy of my enemy is my friend. To put an end to Negan's tyranny, Rick had to ally himself with others, and so an accord was drawn.

Ezekiel closed out his first issue facing a dilemma – should he, Rick and Jesus trust that Dwight wasn't still working for Negan? – but The Kingdom's ruler was still an unknown quantity himself.

ROARR!!

SNARRL!

A MAN'S BEST FRIEND

Former zookeeper Ezekiel had known his Bengal tiger Shiva since birth, as she was born in captivity, presumably at the zoo where he once worked. Ezekiel nursed Shiva when she was wounded, and this formed a strong bond between them. She actually attacked him, but he didn't report it, thus saving her from being put to sleep, further strengthening their connection, and this rapport between them prospered after the apocalypse.

As well as her more obvious assets – strength,

YEAARRRGH!!

ROAARR!

ROAARR!

speed and ferocity – Shiva was fiercely loyal to Ezekiel. This was aided by the fact that she could eat zombie flesh without becoming sick (as Ezekiel informed Michonne after the battle of the Sanctuary) thanks to a tiger's ability to consume carrion, which meant she didn't (always) look on living humans as a potential meal. Ezekiel did keep her chained and she did sleep in a cage, but their affinity was very real, with Shiva fighting alongside Ezekiel against the Saviors. As it happened, Shiva was a key factor in Negan's forces being kept out of the Alexandria Safe-Zone.

"SHIVA ABHORS VIOLENCE. AS DO I." EZEKIEL

IF YOU'RE REALLY *THIS* MUCH OF A *PUSSY*, DO WHAT YOU DO BEST...

...ACT LIKE YOU AREN'T.

FACT FILE

NAME: Ezekiel

AGE: Approximately 50

JOB: Zookeeper (pre-apocalypse), Leader of The Kingdom (post-apocalypse)

FAMILY: Unknown

RELATIONSHIPS POST-APOCALYPSE: Michonne (lover)

LIKES: Shiva, Michonne, Richard, Rick, Jesus (possibly in that order!). Also animals, pacifism, community, the chivalric code

DISLIKES: Violence, tyrants

FIRST APPEARANCE: Issue 108

CURRENT STATUS: Dead (as of issue 144)

DREADLOCKED LOVERS

Even though Michonne isn't a big fan of authority figures, Ezekiel eventually won her over with sheer charm and good will, as well as a bit of flirty swordplay. There's no denying it takes a ballsy man to flirt with an alpha survivor like Michonne.

He eventually trusted her enough to talk to her as himself, rather than as the larger-than-life ruler of The Kingdom, a persona he adopted when he became 'King.' However, Michonne has always responded best to strength. When Ezekiel broke down over the death of Shiva their relationship became more strained, with Michonne calling him – rather ironically given the loss of his feline companion – a "pussy."

AND THIS IS THE REAL YOU?

"YOU SEEM LIKE SOMEONE I CAN TRUST. MIGHT HAVE SOMETHING TO DO WITH HOW DAMN CUTE YOU ARE." EZEKIEL TO MICHONNE

A MAN'S OTHER BEST FRIEND

Ezekiel's head of security, Richard, was his most trusted human companion from The Kingdom. While little of the two men's shared past has been revealed, the depth of feeling between them was clearly evident when Richard was mortally wounded in battle against the Saviors. Ezekiel rushed to his side and tried to reassure him, only for Richard to die in his arms. Ezekiel wept, later revealing to Michonne that he truly regretted not being able to save his friend (issue 119).

THE MEN HAVE ARRIVED. THE BUSES ARE STATIONED OUTSIDE THE GATES AS YOU REQUESTED.

EXCELLENT NEWS! NOW, PLEASE INFORM RICK AND THE OTHERS.

"HOLD ON! YOU'RE GOING TO MAKE IT!" EZEKIEL TO A DYING RICHARD

IT DIDN'T TAKE LONG FOR ME TO REALIZE OUR INITIAL SUCCESS WAS ONLY LUCK.

RICHARD! HOLD ON! YOU'RE GOING TO MAKE IT! YOU'RE GOING TO BE--

> WHAT DO YOU HAVE PLANNED?

> I'M PREPARED TO DO WHATEVER YOU REQUIRE OF ME.

"I CROWNED MYSELF KING OF THIS KINGDOM IN ORDER TO MAKE THE LIVES OF MY PEOPLE AS GOOD AS THEY CAN BE." EZEKIEL ON LEADERSHIP

LEARNING TO RULE

One thing that *The Walking Dead* fans have learned to be wary of is people who assume positions of power in the post-apocalyptic order. Whether it's Negan, the Governor or even the cowardly Gregory, there are too many examples of people exploiting humanity's desperate living conditions to seize control of a group for their own ends. Even if they initially accepted the role grudgingly – as with Rick – power can corrupt even the most honest individuals. On his first encounter with Rick and the others, Ezekiel hardly inspired confidence in them with his bizarre trappings of royalty and regal manner.

However, he may have been deluded and self-important, but Ezekiel's methods and results did seem to be effective and in the best interests of The Kingdom and its inhabitants. Not only did he reject a truce with the Saviors when he learned of their protection racket against the other members of the trade network (including Hilltop), but when an alliance with Alexandria presented itself, he did the right thing and accepted it. After initially only offering advice, the King soon put his money where his mouth was by saving many of the Alexandria survivors from their common enemy the Saviors, including Rick himself. Ezekiel eventually revealed to Michonne, in the aftermath of the attack on the Sanctuary, that the people of The Kingdom were the first real family he'd ever had.

> THIS ISN'T GOING TO GO DOWN LIKE LAST TIME. IT'S JUST NOT.

> YOU'RE DAMN RIGHT.

"THE DAY HAS FINALLY COME TO RIGHT THE WRONGS THAT HAVE BEFALLEN SO MANY PEOPLE UNDER THIS TYRANT." EZEKIEL ALLIES WITH RICK

HIS FINEST HOUR

Freedom and survival are what matters in war. With the trappings of civilized society stripped away, even Ezekiel recognized that he couldn't avoid violence forever.

Without Ezekiel, the Alexandria and Hilltop settlements would surely have been taken by the Saviors. Just at the moment that his oft-protested pacifism looked likely to undermine the efforts of the combined forces against Negan's group, Ezekiel rose from the ashes of his grief over his lost comrades to join them at Hilltop. His finest moments came when the Saviors rammed the Hilltop gates and Ezekiel fought side-by-side with his lover, Michonne, determined to end the bloodshed, but not at the cost of enslavement to the Saviors. True to his principles, once the day was won, Ezekiel returned with his people to The Kingdom – now with Michonne at his side, a new 'tiger' replacing his partner of old.

> DINE! ENJOY THE BOAR WE'VE SLAUGHTERED IN YOUR HONOR!

> EAT AND BE MERRY! FOR TOMORROW WE GO TO WAR!

BLAM! BLAM! BLAM!

I'D LOST SIGHT OF HER IN THE BATTLE. SHE'D TAKEN A FEW MEN OUT-- I THOUGHT SHE WAS PREOCCUPIED WITH THEM.

MAYBE SHE WENT TO FIND ME? MAYBE SHE WAS JUST DRAWN TO THE NOISE.

I WISH SHE'D BEEN CONTENT. I WISH SHE'D NOT COME AFTER ME.

HIS GREATEST SPEECH

"I wish she'd been content. I wish she'd not come after me. There were so many. We were surrounded. But I was able to get away. I turned to call her to me... so we could leave... get away before she was swarmed. She knew there were too many, she knew I'd never get away otherwise. There was no other way. No other way for me to live... I wish I'd died in that field. Coming back here... After losing so many men, I feel embarrassed... ashamed. Things would have been so much better if I had died... My people would see my death as a heroic sacrifice... They'd never have to see me... like this... But most of all, I wouldn't have lost Shiva." Ezekiel offers a eulogy to his feline friend.

HIS DARKEST HOUR

While initially a source of some controversy for many readers, by the time of her death in issue 118 during 'All Out War, Part One,' the loss of Shiva was significant. In her 10 issues, she had, in many ways, come to encapsulate many of *The Walking Dead*'s themes of survival and rebirth in the new world, and it was hard to imagine Ezekiel without her at his side.

Shiva's death showed once and for all that her loyalty to her master went beyond simply following his vocal commands, with Ezekiel being saved from an attacking horde of walkers by his beloved pet. She was overwhelmed by their numbers and made the ultimate sacrifice for Ezekiel. In saving him, Shiva essentially saved The Kingdom from disintegration – that alone is a significant legacy. For his part, Ezekiel truly believed that she was cognizant of the odds against her when she took on the walker herd.

Shiva may have been killed, but Ezekiel retained the kingly principles he'd always tried to exhibit to others. •

I CAN'T DO THIS ANYMORE... I CAN'T LEAD... I CAN'T GO OUT THERE... I JUST CAN'T...

I LEAD THEM TO THE SLAUGHTER... IT WAS MY FAULT...

...AND I CAN'T EVER TAKE THAT BACK... IT... IT CAN'T *EVER* BE UNDONE...

I DON'T... I DON'T...

DEATH SENTENCE

We take a look at those characters who were doomed to end up as worm food as soon as they stepped into frame. They may last one issue, they may appear in several, but they have a 'death sentence' hanging over their heads from the moment we meet them. **WORDS: Dan Auty**

THE CONDEMNED

Ethan lasted a grand total of one issue. He was a resident of the Hilltop community, sent on a mission along with three others to negotiate with the Saviors. We meet him as he returns from this mission alone, shortly after Rick has arrived.

YOU'RE DOOMED

There are various ways to spot an inevitable *Walking Dead* victim. Someone telling a partner or family member they love them shortly before setting off on a dangerous mission. A reckless disregard for orders or safety. Someone covering up a potential wound after an encounter with a walker. But few things spell out a character's looming demise more clearly than to be greeted with the words: "C'mon Ethan — you're safe now." Uh-oh!

AHH… WE LIKED THAT GUY!

We don't have very long to get to know Ethan, but we can ascertain three facts about him before his gruesome demise. He's a clearly a brave and loyal member of Hilltop, having embarked on a dangerous quest to Negan's lair. He and Rick share a similar taste in fur-hooded winter coats. And he has no problem stabbing an old guy in the belly if he thinks it will save a young lady.

NICE KNOWING YA!

After Ethan knifes Gregory in order to save a mystery woman called Crystal, Rick steps in and after a quick grapple in the mud, introduces Ethan to his own blade. Ethan's time in *The Walking Dead* is so fleeting that he's pretty much forgotten by the next page. But at least he avoids being eaten, and is killed by a man with similar tastes in outdoor apparel. •

THE SECRET DIARY OF A WALKER

It's not easy being a zombie in *The Walking Dead* world, as our week in the life/death of an undead walker shows. Diary entries transcribed by Dan Auty…

MONDAY

Getting ready for the annual Walkers' Walk, a charity event that gathers zombies from all over the county. There's a misconception about the term 'walkers;' the fact is, we simply love walking, rambling through the countryside and enjoying a beer and limb platter after a long day on our feet.

TUESDAY

There is concern among some of our members about encountering normos on the walk. I think they remember last year's debacle, when some less dedicated participants stopped to snack on a lost family and barely made it to the finish. It's this sort of behavior that gives us all a bad name.

WEDNESDAY

Training. I'm worried about my ankle. The flesh is long gone and the bone looks distinctly brittle, but I'm hoping it holds. I know it's all for fun, but I don't want to be dragging a gooey stump across the finish line, that would just be way too embarrassing.

THURSDAY

Tomorrow's the big day! Fat Al is joining us. I think it's because Sally's coming, too. Frankly, he hasn't a chance — not only is he a bit too partial to brain sundaes, he's rocking an arm-stump-and-vest look that really isn't her thing. Still, pat on the back for effort…

FRIDAY

Things didn't go quite as planned. Al, Sally and I were enjoying the countryside, stretching what remains of our legs, when from out of nowhere these normos came racing down the lane in a car, sending me and Sally flying and leaving poor old Al as asphalt patty. Barbarians! •

TOP 5
TAKING CHARGE
Top Five Moments of Great Leadership

RICK, PART 1

5. There have been many examples of Rick's great leadership skills over the course of the comic. Equally, there have been many mistakes along the way. But you learn through trial and error. One of Rick's best leadership moments came at the end of the 'All Out War' story arc. Having learned painful lessons from his confrontations with

the Governor, Rick doesn't make the same mistake twice. When he has the opportunity to talk Negan down from continuing the war, he does something that is – if the world hadn't gone to hell – quite shocking.

While Negan is pondering the concept of working together, rather than fighting each other, Rick quickly pulls out a knife and slashes Negan across the throat, deep enough that it would incapacitate his opponent, but not so deep that he couldn't be saved by a good doctor. Negan still has the strength to put up a bit of a fight, but ultimately Rick beats him, capturing his foe alive to make him pay for his crimes and ending the war in one fell swoop. An aggressive tactic for sure, but one that only a strong and perceptive leader such as Rick could have conceived. ◇◇◇◇◇◇

DALE

Dale was a leader with a small 'l.' It was in the little things he did, where he set the standard for doing the right thing and making sure everyone was looking out for one another. He was calm and mild-mannered, if at times a little insecure.

Perhaps Dale's finest moment of leadership, though, was when he took on a paternal role, looking after the children Sophia, Billy and Ben, and taking them away from the dangers of the soon-to-be-overrun prison. In a world where death lurked at every corner, he looked out for them and helped give them at least some sense of safety and stability. Sophia went on to become Glenn and Maggie's adopted

MAGGIE

4. When Gregory, leader of the Hilltop, complains that Rick is making things worse by going to war with Negan, Maggie reminds him what an animal the leader of the Saviors really is. She underlines her point by punching him too – awesome!

But that's not all, this is the moment Maggie takes control of the Hilltop, telling its assembled people that this might be their only chance to beat Negan, and that they need to be onside with Rick. It's a rousing speech that winds up with her as their commander-in-chief forever more. ◇◇◇◇

daughter, and is still alive and well today, mainly thanks to Dale's actions that day at the prison. On the flipside, Ben killed his brother, Billy, but that's another story... ◇◇◇◇◇◇◇◇◇

how to move forward without any further pain. By abiding by his lunatic adversary's demands and staying quiet, Rick made sure that many more people in his community lived to fight another day. And boy, the fight that lay ahead was one hell of a battle...

You could point to Carl's immediate actions after Glenn's death as signs of great leadership, as he stowed away in a Saviors truck, infiltrated the Sanctuary and attempted to assassinate Negan, the man responsible for killing his friend. However, it was also a very rash action – the assault rifle he used was almost as big as him, so there was no way he was going to be able to control the recoil – which later puts his father in a very compromising position. Nice try, kid, but you still have a lot to learn about strategy from your dad. ◇◇◇◇

2. RICK, PART 2

Some would argue that Rick was cowardly in not fighting Negan after the death of Glenn – his own son included. Some might say he should never have let the Saviors take Dwight away after they had captured him either. But there comes a time in the lifespan of a leader where he/she has to accept that they have been beaten, to count their losses, and figure out

1. GLENN

We think Glenn was the series' first true leader. He was always willing to put himself in the firing line, in order to protect the greater good of the group.

Right from the start, he was regularly at the mercy of the undead, as he sought supplies for the group from the zombie-ridden streets of Atlanta. His devotion to the group showed true leadership, as his commitment to their safety and survival never once waned. It was, perhaps, poetic that the show's most foul villain to date – Negan – was the man to swiftly end his life. Glenn represented the force for good, through-and-through. RIP! • ◇◇

MAKING THEIR MARK

The Walking Dead tells the story of Rick Grimes and those around him, most notably Carl, Michonne, Andrea, and Maggie. Indeed, there have been many major characters in the story to date, some still alive and many sadly dead. But the world of *The Walking Dead* is also populated with many minor characters, who have made an impact on Rick's life and, by proxy, the main storyline. Their roles in the narrative are often forgotten — so focused are we on Rick's story — so, *TWDM* decided to dig up the lesser characters who have had an enduring effect on the series.

WORDS: Russell Cook

A t its heart, *The Walking Dead* is a character story. It takes ordinary people like us and throws them into the middle of unbearable situations that often offer no positive outcome. It's these kinds of situations that really get to the crux of humanity, and expose the best (and worst) of how we behave toward one another and how we respond to tragedy and loss.

An apocalyptic story, such as this, requires big personalities but also relatable ones too, to stand out against what is a powerful backdrop. And that's where Robert Kirkman has excelled. From top to bottom, *The Walking Dead* is loaded with memorable and important characters – yet, if you don't pay close attention, you could miss the impact that some of the smaller, seemingly less integral, characters have had on the plot.

Sure, we all root for Rick, Maggie, Michonne, Carl, and so on, but it's worth remembering the part played by the little guy. Sometimes, it's the small acts that have the longest lasting effects, both on the narrative and on us as the reader.

A FIRST TIME FOR EVERYTHING

Amy is the first character to die and, most importantly, it's from a zombie bite. So naturally, her death has a profound impact on the story. The walker attack actually takes place in the early days, when the group were holed up in the Atlanta camp. She's bitten as she makes her way to Dale's RV to use the bathroom, meaning she's infected immediately.

It's a tough moment for the group. But for Andrea, it's doubly difficult. Amy is her younger sister, leaving her faced with one of the story's first examples of an unthinkable situation: putting a bullet between the eyes of a loved one to protect them from becoming undead. It's a huge kick in the teeth for the group, which highlights just how fragile life has become and is a harsh reminder that there's nowhere to hide from the perils of this new world: life and death share the Earth more closely than ever before.

The short-term impact of Amy's death exposes tensions that exist within the group more clearly than at any previous point. While Shane and Rick had been shown to disagree up until this point, Amy's death leads to Rick directly pointing the finger at his former best friend, blaming him for what happened. We really get a flavor here of what the future holds: seemingly small disagreements of opinion can lead to huge repercussions that have a negative impact on the group's stability.

DEATH WISH

Speaking of firsts, Jim – the mechanic who we encounter for the first time in issue two – gives us our earliest insight into the newfound sense of hopelessness that some survivors are feeling. Many of the characters have a willingness and hunger to fight on, but his desire appears to be fading or, perhaps, is lost altogether. During the walker invasion of Atlanta, he lost his entire family and now he feels like there's nothing left to live for anymore.

We all root for Rick, Maggie, Michonne, Carl, and so on, but it's worth remembering the part played by the little guy.

When the Atlanta camp is attacked by walkers, he is bitten on the arm and subsequently infected. Interestingly, both for the reader and the characters, this is the first time we see the prolonged effects of the infection, as he refuses a mercy killing. Instead, when the group vacates the campsite to find a safer place to survive, he chooses to stay behind. He sees zombification as his last chance to be with the family he has lost.

This willingness to passively become one of the undead can be seen as a precursor to the helplessness that Carol feels when she gives herself over to the walkers at the prison. Carol's decline from loving mother to suicidal loner is painful for those who have followed her story from the beginning (especially given how strong a character she is in the TV show). Rejected seemingly by everyone she thought cared for her, she falls into such a deep depression – as Carl says, "she cries a lot" – that even her loving daughter, Sophia, can't save her.

Her actions become increasingly more manic, weird and desperate, until ultimately she decides she doesn't want to go on anymore, sacrificing herself to a tied-up walker. Her final monologue is heartbreaking: "I don't really have

anyone to talk to, so I figured I'd introduce myself. I'm Carol. I think I'll just talk to you from now on. You listen, you don't seem to judge me. That's really important in a friendship, y'know. Not judging people. I really hope you like me... Oh, good... You do like me." Chomp!

Like Jim, Carol's behavior underpins the overarching sense of futility that this new world has brought about. For people like these two, becoming one of the undead is a morbidly welcome comfort.

FIRST DEGREE MURDER

In a world where death is seemingly all there is, it's astonishing to think that the murder of another human being could be seen as a heinous act. Yet, that's precisely how both we, as onlookers, and Tyreese feel about Rick's killing of Dexter in issue 19.

During their tumultuous time together in the prison, Dexter provides a real challenge for Rick. After Dexter openly admits to being a murderer and then later throwing around remarks that come off as threatening toward the group, Rick is forced into new territory: taking the life of another living person in a world where the only enemy should really be the undead roaming the streets.

This, then, is Rick's first *real* kill. The troubling part of it though is the nature of the murder. It was opportunistic and out of character for a man who leads by example and always does the *right* thing. As far as plot devices go, this moment sets a new precedent for what's acceptable. If there's a perceived threat, living or dead, put it down.

What makes this moment particularly compelling is only two issues before, Rick had introduced the death penalty for murder, following the killing spree of Thomas, the serial killer, after he had butchered the Greene twins and sliced up Andrea. In issue 17, Rick pronounced: "You kill. You die." Thomas may have escaped his planned hanging, instead finding death at the hands of Maggie's handgun, but Rick's subsequent murder of Dexter (and let's make no bones about it, this is exactly what it is), even

> Rick's murder of Dexter underlines that there's no room for black and white thinking in this new world.

if it is done for 'the good of the group,' underlines that there's no room for black and white thinking in this new world. Like the artwork of the comic itself, the world is now mostly different shades of gray. As such, Dexter's death marks a clear turning point for Rick.

A SUCCESSFUL OPERATION

Denise may have had a little more 'page time' than the previously mentioned 'little guys' but she's still one of the less celebrated characters in the comic, which is a shame. After

all, she saves Carl's life and, as a result, plays a massive part in shaping the future of Alexandria.

Carl is an integral member of the group, who across the series shows himself to be a key player and, as we know, a leader of sorts. So when you consider his contribution to the story, Denise's actions in saving his life are huge. Carl's survival helps ensure a fragment of hope remains – a rare thing in *The Walking Dead*. He's been around since the beginning and his growth has happened in tandem with the plot. But more than that, Carl has proven to be the motivation that gives Rick, the story's central character, the will to go on and survive. Denise's actions then have a long-lasting impact on the story.

Denise's death happens during 'All Out War,' indirectly through the actions of Negan when he

> **When you consider Carl's contribution to the story, Denise's actions in saving his life are huge.**

returns a zombified Holly back to Alexandria. Holly then bites Denise on the arm, thus sentencing her to death unless she acts fast. But, in keeping with her altruistic personality, Denise opts not to amputate her arm in order to be able to operate on a badly wounded Heath, thus saving his life at the expense of her own.

WHUDD!

NO[T]
WHAT
[I] MEAN[T]

WHAT
ARE YOU
DOING?!

HOLLY, GET
BACK ON THE
BUS BEFORE
THEY START
SHOOTING
AGAIN!

HOLLY!

Holly is an interesting minor character, who also makes the decision to sacrifice herself to save another.

HOLLY!

YOU THINK
I'D LET YOU
GET OFF THAT
FUCKING EASY,
DID YOU?
NO
FUCKING
WAY,
SISTER.

TROJAN HORSE

Holly herself is an interesting minor character, who also makes the decision to sacrifice herself to save another, in this case Rick. From her relationship with Abraham and assistance in keeping Alexandria safe to standing shoulder-to-shoulder with Rick during 'All Out War,' she leaves a lasting mark on *The Walking Dead*.

The first of her two biggest moments comes in issue 116 when she refuses to let Rick sacrifice himself by driving a vehicle through the walls of the Saviors' compound, the Sanctuary. She recognizes his vital importance to the group, so she jumps in the truck herself and ploughs straight into the heart of the enemy's base, allowing a horde of walkers to storm Negan's stronghold, causing mayhem. We can't help but think that she didn't plan on surviving this, so it is perhaps a surprise to both her and the reader when she is captured alive by Negan (who interestingly mistakes her for Andrea). It's through Holly that we also find out that Negan has some peculiar morals: he's more than happy to subjugate others, but won't stand for rape, despite having a 'forced' harem of his own.

Several issues later, the Saviors bring her back to Alexandria, only there's a twist: unbeknown to the group (she has a bag over her head), Holly is now a walker and, as previously mentioned, takes a bite out of Denise's arm. Sadly for Holly, she is very quickly killed and consigned to the history books.

SETTING A POOR EXAMPLE

Finally, it's worth mentioning Gregory. As one-time leader of the Hilltop – a colony that on paper is an ally – Gregory's among an elite group that includes Rick, Ezekiel, and Negan. Yet quite frankly, the man's a coward. It's because of this though that he's a memorable character. He gives us something to rally against and presents the image of a leader who acts only out of self-preservation.

He provides Maggie Greene with the perfect opportunity to rebuild – at this

I WON'T TAKE THIS FROM YOU! NOT AFTER EVERYTHING I'VE BEEN THROUGH-- NOT AFTER EVERYTHING I'VE SACRIFICED!

I LAID MY *LIFE* ON THE LINE TO SAVE THESE PEOPLE-- TO BRING THEM HOME! I'M DOING EVERYTHING I CAN TO KEEP EVERYONE SAFE.

Gregory gives us something to rally against and presents the image of a leader who acts only out of self-preservation.

to regain control of the Hilltop in issue 137. His attempt ultimately fails and he is locked up for a few issues, protesting his innocence. Maggie is initially unwilling to kill the incarcerated Gregory, but eventually decides that his manipulation of the colonists to turn them against her and his murder attempt must be met by death. Proving once and for all that she's a far more decisive leader than Gregory, he is hanged in issue 142, presumably in front of all the Hilltop inhabitants.

point in time, she's still trying to recover from the death of her beloved, Glenn. Gregory's everything that Maggie isn't. She's stared down the worst of both humanity and the undead right in the face, and is still alive in the comic today to tell the tale. Gregory is essentially the vehicle for her ascension to leadership; she takes over control of the Hilltop community with Gregory still alive.

Following the defeat of the Saviors, Gregory seals his own fate when he attempts to poison Maggie

WHAT DID YOU DO? YOU--

DID YOU FUCKING POISON ME?! DID YOU--

By delivering such complicated 'minor' characters, *The Walking Dead* manages to have a seemingly endless lifespan. Indeed, if we tracked back and dug around even further we're certain that even more prophetic gems, hinting at the future of the series, would surface. But for now, let's remember what these characters have given to the story, both in terms of individual contribution and their effect on the behaviour of those around them.

So good or bad, let's hear it for the little guy! •

THIS IS ABSURD. THIS--THIS SIMPLY CAN'T BE HAPPENING. YOU CAN'T KEEP ME LOCKED IN HERE. I'M.. I'LL DIE. DON'T DO THIS!

SOMETHING TO FEAR

With Rick and co settling into a life of semi-normalcy in the Alexandria Safe-Zone, writer Robert Kirkman knew it was time to shake things up in *The Walking Dead* comic. Enter Negan. Leader of a large, well-armed group of survivors, known as the Saviors, Negan fast becomes *someone* to fear. Let's find out why. WORDS: Stuart Barr

NEGAN ISN'T GOING TO LIKE THIS...

Volume 16, 'A Larger World,' significantly expanded *The Walking Dead* playground. Since the beginning, it had been centered around Rick, his family, the small band around them and their day-to-day struggle for survival. The hermetic boundaries of this existence began to dissolve when they arrived at the Alexandria Safe-Zone and integrated into an established community. They were then blown apart by the arrival of Paul 'Jesus' Monroe, an emissary of the more established Hilltop colony. The Safe-Zone community thought they were a microcosm, self-contained and alone, but now they are a microcosm among a group of communities in the DC area.

Monroe wishes to set up trade routes not only between Alexandria and Hilltop, but with other, as yet, unnamed communities. Lacking a supply surplus or significant produce production to trade, Rick offers their combat experience to help defend against the Saviors, a bandit group who regularly raid the communities led by a mysterious figure known as Negan.

> Rick is doing what a leader must, taking decisive action in pursuit of the greater good... In a post-apocalyptic Washington, politics is reborn.

Monroe is a capable fighter and skilled scout, but the denizens of Hilltop are ill-equipped and inexperienced. In Rick, Abraham, Michonne, Andrea and the rest, Monroe sees battle-hardened survivors and maybe even a leader to boot.

Rick's unilateral decision to barter the group's combat experience was not universally welcomed, with Glenn seeing the Hilltop as an idyllic commune, Michonne reacting with suspicion (the volume title, 'Something To Fear,' describing her default reaction to the unfamiliar), while Andrea was contemptuous of their lack of combat readiness. In political terms, Glenn is the dove, Andrea the hawk, and Michonne the paranoid center.

Rick is doing what a leader must, taking decisive action in pursuit of the greater good, but he now must develop diplomatic skills. It is one thing to lead a group, but a different proposition to broker agreement and influence other groups. In a post-apocalyptic Washington, politics is reborn.

After collecting supplies from Monroe, Rick's party is held up by a small group of Saviors. All answer to the name 'Negan' and it may be that Rick initially believes he is facing their leader. Michonne's katana and Andrea's rifle deal with the gang, while Rick sends the sole survivor running for the hills with a message to Negan: there is a new sheriff in town.

In the Safe-Zone, the group has had time to strengthen its bonds. Glenn discovers his partner, Maggie Greene, is pregnant. Rick and Andrea have become romantically involved; Carl discovers them in bed together and although he does not say it, it is clear that he is happy for his father. The relationship between Eugene Porter and Rosita Espinosa is at an early stage: his initial attempts to woo Abraham's ex are hampered by feelings of masculine inadequacy. This leads him to taunt Abraham, falsely claiming he and Rosita are physically intimate. While these relationships give Rick's group

something to lose and a reason to fear, they also give them something to protect.

Eugene has identified locations where equipment may be found to manufacture precious ammunition. Embarrassed by his attempt to assert masculine dominance over Abraham, he asks him to accompany him on a scout. Abraham explains to Eugene that while he still has feelings for Rosita, he holds no ill will and wishes them the best. During this heart-to-heart, Abraham is struck and killed by a crossbow bolt and dies in mid-sentence.

This is a shocking death because the victim is among the strongest characters in *The Walking Dead,* and because it happens so quickly. Robert Kirkman has indicated that this plot development was not planned in advance, but it perfectly captures the senseless and arbitrary nature of conflict. Abraham is there one moment and then just gone, like a prayer in a foxhole. There is no warning, no villain's

Abraham's death perfectly captures the arbitrary nature of conflict... There is no warning, no villain's monologue. The death has a sudden and brutal finality.

IN A NUTSHELL

TITLE: Something To Fear
FEATURED ISSUES: 97-102
COLLECTION: Volume 17
SYNOPSIS: Following a meeting with Paul Monroe, a representative of anothe[r] survivor colony called the Hilltop, Rick decides to offer his group's services as muscle in a trade for supplies. While o[n] the way to Hilltop to finalize the deal, h[e] Carl, Michonne, Heath, Glenn, Maggie [and] Sophia are captured by a brutal group o[f] bandits calling themselves the Saviors [.] Negan is their leader and, as he quickl[y] proves, he's not someone to be trifled w[ith]

TIDBITS:

- There's only one place to start: the de[ath] of Glenn. To say this was a shock is somewhat of an understatement; his was one of the most surprising death[s] in the series. His cold-blooded murde[r at] the hands of Negan, which is drawn o[ut] over five pages, caused genuine outra[ge] among many fans, who were stunned to lose a character who had been in t[he] series since the very start. It almost made you forget, Abraham had died o[nly] a few issues earlier... Almost.

- Despite a show of having scruples, Negan ultimately decides who to kill [by] using the tried and trusted schoolyar[d] technique of "Eeny, meeny, miny moe [...] Catch a tiger by the toe" – a foretelli[ng] of the introduction of Shiva, perhaps[?]

- Series artist Charlie Adlard has state[d] that, from a purely artistic point of vi[ew] he was glad that Glenn was finally kil[led] off: he always found him a very difficu[lt] character to illustrate.

- Negan (pronounced 'Knee-gan) is definitely the foulest-mouthed charac[ter] in the comic. In his first encounter wi[th] Rick, he uses the 'eff' word 41 times, including this rather choice phrase, "[I'm] now going to beat the holy fuck fuckin[g] fuckedy fuck out of one of you with m[y] bat." It's clear Robert Kirkman has gr[eat] fun writing Negan's dialogue.

- This volume sees Maggie and Sophia stay behind in Hilltop. Maggie will go [on] to become the community's leader dur[ing] the epic 'All Out War' arc.

Negan is like many warlords found in real-world conflict zones. He's a gangster who's conned and muscled his way into power.

monologue. The death has a sudden, brutal and very *Walking Dead* finality.

The bolt was fired by Dwight, a distinctively burned Savior who has been leading a war party scouting the Safe-Zone. He weighs up Eugene and decides he isn't a threat, instead taking him hostage and demanding that the compound's gate be opened. It's a schoolboy error – Eugene bites Dwight's crotch, allowing Rick to open fire. In the melee, most of the Saviors are killed but Dwight escapes. Rick pursues, but when he discovers Abraham, the corpse has attracted walkers and he is forced to abandon the chase.

Rick needs more information; believing that they are safe from another attack, he forms a party to travel to Hilltop and find out more about their adversaries. Fearing for his family and believing the larger community offers more safety, Glenn announces he will stay behind in Hilltop with Maggie and their unborn child. Andrea is ready to accompany Rick, but he asks her to stay behind to organize defenses in case of a Savior attack.

On the way to Hilltop, the party stop to make camp. That night a group of Saviors, led by Negan, take them by surprise. This is the event the whole volume has been building up to (and neatly arrives for the landmark issue 100). This event sets the tone for a massive story that runs right up to issue

126, with Negan attaining 'Big Bad' status. Negan understands theatre, and his first appearance is not one any who survive it will forget. A tall, physically imposing man with jet-black slicked-back hair, Negan wears a uniform of jeans and black leather biker jacket.

While we were given small crumbs of information about the Governor's life pre-zombie holocaust, we never really find out anything about Negan. This gives him a frightening unpredictability. Where the Governor was insane, talking to zombie heads in fish tanks and living

Negan commits atrocities with a clear motive and for a set purpose. It is entirely possible Negan actually believes he is justified.

The captives are introduced to 'Lucille,' a barbed wire wrapped baseball bat and Negan's weapon of choice. Negan's habit of addressing Lucille as a girlfriend could be a sign of madness, but it could also just be part of his act. While clearly a sadist with a personality disorder, if tried in a court of law, it's unlikely Negan could plead insanity. He commits atrocities but with a clear motive and for a set purpose. It is entirely possible Negan actually believes he is justified.

Savoring the fear of those kneeling before him, Negan chooses Glenn from the line-up and beats him to death with Lucille. "He's taking it like a champ," he cackles as the dying young man attempts to stand. It is worth noting that despite the extreme brutality of this act, which is among the most shocking deaths in *The Walking Dead* (along with Lori and Judith back in issue 48), Negan does let slip one of his scruples. Initially, as he moves down the row of kneeling prisoners selecting a sacrificial lamb, he appears to rule Glenn out on the basis of race. However, he can't kill Rick as that would create a martyr, he won't kill Maggie as she is pregnant, he won't kill Carl as he is just a boy. He is not above joking that he might have Carl raped, however, something that sits at odds with a later episode where he executes one of his own for sexual assault.

Glenn's brutal and senseless death – and the powerlessness of the group to stop the act – has a significant impact. Once

with his dead daughter, Negan shows signs of madness, but often undercuts this with knowing winks to his audience (Negan loves an audience) that suggest he's playing a calculated role.

Back to the story: Rick and his group are tied and forced to kneel while Negan explains he wants half of Alexandria's supplies. This is presented as a 'deal' but is really an ultimatum. He also wants revenge for the men killed by Rick's group.

Subsequent volumes will reveal the extremity of Negan's cult-like leadership style, but it is arguable whether his revenge is at all personal or rather a showcase for his followers. One of the traits that makes Negan so hard to read (in a metaphysical sense) is his sense of humor; he has a fondness for wisecracks as black as his hair.

In political terms, Glenn is the dove, Andrea the hawk, and Michonne the paranoid center.

YOU WANT TO DO **WHAT?!**

What Rick does next is controversial: he tells the community they cannot win. He advises submitting to Negan and releasing Dwight. The night before, Rick sought counsel from Michonne, who, to his surprise, agreed. She is tired of killing and still harbors guilt over her actions against the Governor which provoked the prison massacre. Andrea is less understanding, but eventually accepts this plan of action. Secretly, Rick is formulating a long-term plan: when Dwight is released, he sends Monroe to tail him, in order to locate the Savior base and return with intelligence about the new enemy.

This is a battle lost, but the war has barely begun. •

released, they travel on towards Hilltop where Glenn is buried, and Maggie elects to remain behind with Sophia. Rick confronts the Hilltop leaders and discovers that their knowledge of the Saviors is slight; they were unaware of their numbers and had never met Negan. The fact that the Savior leader felt the need to confront Rick personally is evidence he has recognized a significant threat.

Negan is like many warlords found in real-world conflict zones. He's a gangster who's conned and muscled his way into power. Skilled in identifying and exploiting the weaknesses of others, his real goal (whether conscious or not) is a comfortable life. However, he believes himself to be honest and a man of his word. It is in Negan's best interests that the communities he raids remain productive, healthy and terrified. He does not kill Rick for the very reason that it could lead to rebellion. Negan wants to allow the communities autonomy; he needs what they have, and he needs a constant supply of it.

Leaving Maggie and Sophia behind, and taking Monroe with them, Rick's group return to Alexandria to discover the Saviors have assaulted the compound. Andrea successfully led a defense and the Saviors lost another dozen or so men. Dwight has been captured and Andrea is eager to execute him for Abraham's murder even before she finds out about Glenn. This is little comfort to Rick, who knows that Negan has enough men to overwhelm the community. It's not a fight he can win and Rick knows it.

PACK UP NOW, WHILE EVERYONE IS DISTRACTED. HIT THE ROAD BEFORE IT'S TOO HARD TO CATCH UP TO HIM.

I NEED TO KNOW WHAT WE'RE UP AGAINST. FIND OUT EVERYTHING YOU CAN ABOUT NEGAN AND HIS PEOPLE... AND REMEMBER, FOR THEIR SAKE, *NO ONE* CAN KNOW WHAT WE'RE REALLY DOING HERE.

DEATH SENTENCE

Remember that character who was doomed as soon as they stepped into frame? No? Us either! So our 'Death Sentence' feature is here to remind us. WORDS: Dan Auty

THE CONDEMNED

Donnie is quick to appear, and even quicker to depart. He's one of Negan's men, and when the Saviors begin their final assault on Hilltop, he finds himself within its gates.

Taking up a position on one of the outer walls, Donnie gets ready to shoot at any enemies he sees coming his way.

SHARP SHOOTIN'

We don't learn that much about Donnie while he is still alive. At first, he's merely a tiny silhouette on a high wall, as Eugene, Carson, and some others head to Hilltop in a stolen van. When Carson turns on the van's headlights we finally see him — and within seconds he's opened fire, stopped the van dead in its tracks and, so he thinks, maybe killed those inside.

THIS CHARMING MAN

Donnie doesn't get much of a chance to speak before his untimely demise, but it's enough to see that he went to the same charm school as Negan. Listening to the drone of the crashed van's horn down below, he announces to no-one in particular: "Lay on the horn all fucking night, retard! Those undead fucks ain't going nowhere!" Charming!

GOT WHUDD!

He may be quite a good marksman, but smart Donnie is not. Eugene and co have no problem climbing up on the wall while he is gloating about the damage he's caused their van. The normally mild-mannered Eugene then does something unexpected — he throws a startled Donnie into a horde of ravenous walkers. Eugene is initially upset, this being the first man he has killed, but Carson assures him that Donnie was not a nice man. "Fuck him then," Eugene replies quite reasonably. Night-night, Donnie! ●

THE SECRET DIARY OF A WALKER

It's not easy being a zombie in *The Walking Dead* world, as our week in the life/death of an undead walker proves. Diary transcribed by Stuart Barr…

MONDAY

I remember before. I'd wake up, maybe find a plastic spaceship stuck to my face. Think about going to work at the call center. Phoning people about accident insurance. Get sworn at. Sigh! I'd rather have been playing *Cosmic Encounter*.

TUESDAY

Trying to get a D&D game set up. Zombies are the worst. All they want to play is *Operation* or *Pin The Lower Intestine On The Donkey*. Got some beers and a bucket with a family in it. They ate the family, drank the beer and left. One of them even took the bucket as a hat. Sigh! I'd rather be playing *Cosmic Encounter*.

WEDNESDAY

Amazing! Found the *Cosmic Encounter* box under the bed while looking for rats to eat. All the pieces are there. Finding it hard to shuffle the cards now. Used to be able to roll a mean D20, now I can barely pick up a D6. Roommate came home with his loud pals. They have party hats and mixed entrails. Sigh! I wish we were playing *Cosmic Encounter*.

THURSDAY

Going out, still visit the comic shop on main street. The warm mouth-breathers raid the other stores, but leave the zombie comics alone. Seem to have gone out of fashion. I like them. Kitchen sink drama these days. But… I'd rather be playing *Cosmic Encounter*.

FRIDAY

Some warm mouth-breathers are in town, think I'll go check them out. There's a guy with a mullet and another with a comedy mustache. Maybe they would like to play *Cosmic Encounter*? Ulp! ●

TOP 5

BRAINS AND BRAWN
Negan's Top Five Best Moments

5. STRIKE OUT

At the end of his tenure as the series' biggest asshole, The Governor kills a major character. In issue 100, Negan begins his reign of terror by dispatching one: Glenn, one of the series' most-beloved characters. It's the way Negan does it too, smashing a barb wire-covered baseball bat – which he lovingly refers to as Lucille – repeatedly into our hero's head. Harsh stuff. The act is a big statement and a moment that opens the door to a new and even darker chapter in the story.

4. MIND GAMES

Negan proves himself to be a master of manipulation, not least after finding Carl stowed away in one of his trucks. As their captor/captive relationship unfolds, and switches over time, it becomes indicative of the changing shape of *The Walking Dead*'s world. Physical prowess counts, but controlling feelings and emotions is proving to be more powerful. So, when Negan finally releases Carl to Rick in issue 107, it's a bit of a shock to all. This is a man who knows how to rule and get what he wants, without always resorting to the lowest common denominator to achieve it. It's a sign of his intelligence and another reason why he's a far greater villain than his predecessor.

3. HONOR KILL

When Spencer comes to Negan to make a claim for the leadership of Alexandria, little does he know that it will be the death of him. He calls for Rick's head and displays a trait that the tyrant loathes above all else: cowardice. Negan tells him he "has no guts" before ironically slashing his stomach open, killing him. It's a dark moment, but one that commands at least the tiniest bit of respect for our new villain. In Rick, Negan sees a real man who will die for the good of his people. In Spencer he sees a traitor. It's yet another moment that makes us, as the reader, feel conflicted.

2. INNOVATION IS KEY

Some of history's greatest (if you can even refer to them as that) villains pushed society to question and think differently about things, albeit indirectly for the most part. In some cases, in a screwed-up kind of way, they even played their part in advancing the realms of technological understanding. Now, we're not saying Negan's smearing-of-the-weapons-with-zombie-entrails in issue 122 is hugely innovative or that it helped society move forward in any way, but it is surprising that nobody thought of it as an added means of defense beforehand. Through his sick desire to rule and kill those that get in his way, he manages to come up with a new type of weaponry: zombie guts-infused ones. In a way, that's impressive, right? Listen, don't get angry with us, we're just saying…

1. MIXED EMOTIONS

Why Negan decides to save Holly from the teeth of a biter in issue 116 may never be known. The fact is, he does do this, and Holly lives to see another day. This adds, again, to the mounting evidence that Negan isn't truly all bad. But then, is this part of the 'game' that Rick believes villain *número uno* is playing with them all? Who really knows?! From killing Glenn, to capturing and then releasing Carl, to saving Holly – it is so confusing. Should fans hate him or what? Just stop it, Negan! We need things to be in black and white like the images on the comic page. Either way, the ambiguous nature of Negan's personality makes for one hell of a character, let alone a villain. ◇◇◇◇◇

SAVE YOURSELF

TWDM'S Guide To The Saviors

TWDM takes an in-depth look at another fearsome survivor group, the Saviors, who gave Rick and the gang some major headaches in the sixth and seventh seasons of the AMC show.
WORDS: Sam Faulkner

"Near as I can tell, they're a roaming band of maniacs on an unending killing spree... Word is they've killed thousands of the dead already." **Jesus**

Rick and his group of survivors have been through some extremely tough times. As if the hordes of walkers who have infested the world weren't enough to contend with, they have been through internal strife, betrayal, and a power-mad dictator in the form of the Governor. Alexandria appears to be a paradise at first, a safe place with a walled-in community all working together to make it through a terrifying new world. That doesn't last though, as soon a major threat comes knocking at the door.

The Saviors are an intimidating group of survivors, made up of physically capable and loose-principled members. They are a powerful and large group, relying on fear and shock tactics to maintain their iron grip over the various nearby settlements. Formed by a dangerous man named Negan, the group has fallen into a pattern of violence and intimidation as they stalk the area, forcing weaker survivors to subsidize them with supplies that they demand as payment for 'protection.' They are an organized, nasty, and well-resourced gang with bad intentions. Simply put, they are the bully boys of *The Walking Dead*.

MOB TACTICS

The Saviors are made up of particularly combat proficient members, well skilled in the art of walker extermination. They typically arrive at a settlement, clear out the undead menace from the immediate locale, and then demand payment for their efforts. This payment is usually vastly disproportionate, often leaving an innocent, more peaceful settlement suffering from desperate shortages of supplies as a result of the Saviors' strong-arming. The psychological effect of a well-armed group of antagonistic humans arriving at the gates is clear, with even Rick temporarily bending to their demands – though as many adversaries have found throughout the series' run, pushing Rick is never a good idea.

Negan himself is a far more complex character than he initially appears, so memorably in issue 100. Cruel, violent, and unpredictable, with a very clear lust for power and domination over those physically weaker than himself, Negan is nevertheless a charismatic and intelligent presence. Speaking in an aggressive, brash tone, using 'colorful' humor to cover his sadistic nature, he clearly revels in the brute power of his own presence. And you thought the Governor was an egomaniac!

Alexandria is a peaceful yet fragile settlement, and the appearance of this imposing, leather-jacketed man spouting profanities and threats in an off-hand, jokey manner is unsettling for the Alexandrians, to say the least. His casual approach to brutality is evident – Negan leads from the front, taking part in the elimination of a group of walkers with apparent glee. He seems to actively enjoy

dispatching the walkers, but takes an even more ruthless approach to 'thinkers,' later smearing walker remains on his army's handheld weapons and projectiles to ensure infection of any targets who receive an injury in combat.

Negan has been known to show a certain amount of mercy – though rarely in the name of humanity. For instance, he spares Carl after the boy kills several members of his group: it is an unexpected move, but is done for self-serving reasons, namely trying to keep Rick in line, as well as the suggestion that perhaps he views Carl as a future protégé. Glimmers of some rudimentary form of moral code do shine through, such as his stepping in to spare Alexandrian captive Holly from a brutal assault at the hands of one of his crew, insisting he does not approve of sexual violence. He tries to assure Holly that the Saviors aren't "monsters." Barely an issue later, he then kills Holly (unseen by the reader) and uses her reanimated corpse to try to incite horror and inflict damage (she bites the Alexandrians' doctor, Denise) on Rick's group.

the count falls on Glenn, one of the comic book's most horribly memorable sequences ensues as the man is beaten graphically to death in front of his wife, Maggie, and friends. It's an inglorious way for Glenn to go out, and does little to win Negan anything other than contempt.

The aforementioned weapon is Lucille. Negan's personal instrument of violence and probably the most notorious weapon in the entire series, Lucille is a heavy wooden slugger, wrapped in barbed wire and wielded with enthusiasm. Over the course of the Saviors arc, Lucille becomes something of a symbol of both Negan's oppression and his dangerous magnetism – his reaction when a chunk of 'her' is shot off is very telling, as he demands Carl pay for it, despite having had a slightly more sympathetic relationship with the boy than other characters.

BAT OUT OF HELL

Negan underlines his ruthless nature the first time we meet him. It's hard to agree with a warped code of ethics that sees him offer the hand of peace while at the same time cold-bloodedly battering Glenn, one of the series' most beloved characters, to death with a disturbingly personalized baseball bat. The infamous scene in issue 100, in which Negan holds several members of the group at his mercy, before 'eenie meenie'-ing his way to a decision on who to kill, is unbearably tense. When

"This is a lady. But at times, yeah, she ain't so nice. Truth is… Lucille is a bitch. But she's my bitch." Negan

RULING WITH AN IRON FIST… AND AN IRON!

The fortified settlement that the Saviors call home is known as the Sanctuary. It is an old industrial building, gruesomely decorated with dead walkers around the walls, and 'live' ones chained up and ready to munch on any unwanted trespassers. This makes the settlement an effective fortress, almost unapproachable from the outside thanks to the decomposing wall of gnashing teeth on all sides. It's a neat metaphor for the Saviors – an imposing, frightening structure on the apocalyptic landscape, and that's even before you see the unsettling interior.

Inside, there's a disquieting feeling of normality about the lifestyle the Saviors have adopted – and it's all built around Negan. There's an almost cult-like atmosphere to the place, with Negan revered and feared in equal measure. The community lives on a bizarre points system, being awarded privileges based on how much they have pleased or displeased their leader. Members bow as he passes, recite his words as a chant, and are encouraged to show utmost loyalty to him under pain of physical reprisals. These come to a nasty head whenever one of Negan's subjects is judged to have wronged him, receiving a permanent reminder of their sins through vicious burns to their face thanks to a hot iron. This is one of those occasions where the undead menace outside the

THE BURN IDENTITY

Dwight is another major player in the group's dynamic, leading raiding parties on missions outside the Sanctuary and acting as reluctant second-in-command to Negan. Their relationship is, to say the least, strained. That Negan has taken Dwight's partner, Sherry, as one of his own 'wives' is a cause of festering resentment in the latter, and the heavy facial scarring Negan inflicted on him does little to help matters.

This is not to say that Dwight is squeaky-clean himself – he fires the arrow which kills Abraham at the beginning of the conflict between the Saviors and Rick's group, and seems intent on harming Carl before Negan stops him. So Dwight is not the purest of characters, but he does play a major part in the ultimate downfall of his leader. Along with Negan's other assorted enemies, the Saviors leader has fostered a raging resentment among several of his own men. When all of his self-made enemies gather to face him down, there is little Negan can do to save himself from a downfall of his own making.

In classic dictatorial style, Negan's regime of oppression and fear

"The fastest way to a man's heart is through his vagina." Negan

walls becomes very much a secondary horror.

One member we see mutilated for a perceived sin is being punished for consorting with a former lover, who is now one of Negan's 'wives.' As if the Savior's leader wasn't already very clearly a villain, we find out he also keeps an indentured harem of women he has collected over time. Clearly, Tinder is a thing of the past in the post-apocalyptic world of *The Walking Dead*, and this is not a good way of finding true love. Indeed, as he rules over his unfortunate group, more than one man in the group has been found guilty of getting a little too close. This was the fate that scarred Negan's not-so trusted lieutenant, Dwight.

"We don't have to be afraid of him or his rules anymore. Things will be better, now. You'll see."
Dwight

"The screams are nice but I want to see the blood and the bone." **Negan**

I'LL TELL YOU HIS SECRETS, HIS WEAKNESSES... I'LL BRING YOU THAT ASSHOLE'S *HEAD* ON A SILVER PLATTER...

...AND *THEN* IT WON'T MATTER IF YOU TRUST ME... BECAUSE THAT MOTHERFUCKER WILL BE *DEAD.*

AND THIS NIGHTMARE WILL, AT LONG LAST, BE *OVER.*

NOT ONE WORD TO NEGAN ABOUT ANY OF THIS. NOT ONE DAMN WORD.

AGREED.

eventually puts too much pressure on the people beneath him, and it is Dwight who energizes a revolution of sorts. Forming a hastily assembled militia, Dwight plays a major part in the conflict between Negan and Rick, eventually helping to take down his former leader. Rick shows mercy on Negan, taking him prisoner rather than finishing off his stricken enemy – an act of lingering civility, which Negan is quick to deride as a weakness. This classical unbalanced alpha male still rages and resists, even after defeat, showing that the survivors may never be truly safe from the influence of men like him.

AFTER THE FALL

After some time has passed, Negan becomes something of an enigmatic presence. Still clearly resenting Rick, he is shown to have developed a bizarre kinship with Carl. Living in captivity in a cell in Rick's basement after the events of 'All Out War' is a far cry from his former life as the master and commander of a large group of fawning followers and reluctant wives.

He is, as Rick observes, 'neutered,' but some glimmer of his former power does remain in the group of his former soldiers, now under the command of Dwight. There's certainly a hint that Negan is just biding his time until the perfect opportunity comes to escape from Rick's jail and reassert his dominance over the nearby communities.

In the meantime, the Saviors have become a more integrated part of the community of survivors under Rick's overall

> ## "I'm here because after everything you did... I'm the only thing you can use to convince yourself you're a good person."
> **Negan to Rick**

command. With Dwight as their leader, the Saviors are still a major force to be reckoned with, but with their tainted past as *The Walking Dead*'s Mafiosa, and continuing bubbling resentment toward Rick and Dwight, their future may not be such a rosy one... •

TOP 5

GLENN & MAGGIE SCENES
Counting down the Five Great Glenn & Maggie Moments

FIRST ENCOUNTER

Glenn and Maggie Greene remain two of our favorite characters in the comic. Although Glenn is no longer with us, his impact is still being felt very much today in the comic, with Maggie always mindful of the memory of her murdered husband. Their first encounter was an interesting one. It happened at the Greene family farm in issue 10: after dinner, Maggie follows Glenn out onto the stoop, where she questions him about his feelings for Carol, who has become Tyreese's lover. He bemoans the fact that everyone else seems to be pairing up except for him. The 19-year-old Maggie's response is direct and to the point: "I'll fuck you. If that's what you're after, I'll fuck you." Glenn would have to be stupid to turn down an offer like that.

Following this frank admission, Glenn and Maggie start to sneak around Hershel's farm like naughty teenagers, looking for any opportunity to copulate. It all ends in tears (and lots of shouting) when Hershel discovers his daughter in bed with Glenn soon after the death of two of his other children. He understandably goes crazy. Eventually, Hershel comes to accept them as a couple and even presides over the marriage, but it's not the most auspicious of starts to a relationship. ◇◇◇

4. HAPPY SEXY FUN TIMES

Young couples need their privacy for… well, you know. Unfortunately, fighting for survival in the zombie apocalypse doesn't afford much opportunity for 'sexy times,' but in issue 15, Glenn and Maggie find themselves alone in the prison's barbershop, away from prying eyes, not least those of Maggie's father, Hershel. OK, so it's not the most romantic of locales, but that doesn't seem to trouble Maggie, who proclaims, "Hmm. Never done it in a barber's chair before." The saucy minx! It's time to get it on – all they really need is some Barry White. Somewhere along the way, they also manage to find time to cut each other's hair – we're not sure what that says about Glenn's staying power! ◇◇◇◇◇◇◇◇◇◇◇◇◇◇

3. DON'T LEAVE ME HANGIN'

Issue 55 was one of the darkest hours in Maggie and Glenn's relationship. Devastated by the death of her father and last-surviving brother and riddled with guilt and regret, Maggie decides to end it all and hangs herself. It's only thanks to the quick intervention of Glenn, with the help of Abraham, that she is quickly cut down. However, when it looks like she's died, Abe wants to put a bullet in her head to stop her returning. Rick stops him, and Maggie ultimately gasps back into life.

It's in the aftermath of this event that we see just how strong Glenn and Maggie's relationship has become. It takes time (five issues, no less) for them to eventually talk about the incident, but Maggie finally admits to her husband that it was a moment of weakness that led to her decision to end her life, and she immediately regretted making it. It also made her realize that despite all of the horror, she wants to make a life for herself with Glenn and their adopted daughter, Sophia. "You make life, even this life, worth living, Glenn," she says. "I love you." If you aren't welling up while reading this scene, then you need to take a good hard look at yourself. ◇◇◇◇

2. "I WANT TO LEAVE."

OK, so you're all wondering why we've not included in this list the death of Glenn at the hands of Negan, in front of his pregnant wife and daughter. An earth-shattering moment that ends Glenn and Maggie's relationship forever. Well, the truth is we wanted this list to be a celebration of the couple rather than a dirge, and so have focused on the positives. This particular moment happens in issue 99, with Glenn convincing Maggie to move from Alexandria to the Hilltop, setting in motion events that will eventually lead to Glenn's demise.

So, is this a positive moment? We like to think so. Although it starts with an argument, it ends with the couple being as close as they have ever been. Glenn is full of hope for the future, believing Hilltop is a safer environment for his wife and children

to live, survive and thrive in. Maggie is not as convinced, but she tells him she loves and trusts him, adding: "Wherever you go, I'll follow." As it turns out, it's a terrible decision, but then hindsight is a beautiful thing. At least in this quiet moment of calm before the storm, we are given a glimmer of hope and a touching portrayal of how deep their love is for each other. ◇◇◇◇◇◇◇◇◇◇

1. GETTING HITCHED

Getting married is a momentous day in any couple's lives and although, given the choice, they might have decided not to marry in a prison canteen in lovely orange jail garb, with a retired vet for a priest and a congregation of misfits, some of whom they barely know, it's still one of the happiest moments ever depicted in the comic. After seeking the approval of Hershel, Glenn goes down on bended knee in issue 36. Rather brilliantly, Maggie says she needs to think about it, leaving Glenn hanging with a terrified look on his face, before laughingly accepting and telling him he's an idiot for not realizing she was kidding.

The wedding itself takes place in the following issue, as described above. The happy couple have prepared their own vows. Glenn is clearly nervous, stumbling over his words, but the sentiment is clear: "I vow to love you for as long as I have left and do everything in my power to ensure that is a long time." Maggie is more confident in her response: "I pledge to share my life with you. Whether the days to come are happy or sad, I will live them with you." Awwww! **TW** ◇◇◇

THE MAD, THE BAD

AND THE DANGEROUS TO KNOW

At *TWDM* we often talk about the 'hero' archetype, but what about the flip side? What does being a 'villain' in *The Walking Dead* actually mean? *TWDM* investigates the darker side of humanity. **WORDS:** Dan Auty

Anyone who has read *The Walking Dead* for more than a couple of issues will know that the walkers are not the bad guys. While it's true that the threat they pose informs virtually every decision made by the characters, the living dead, for the most part, are predictable and manageable. If everyone in this world got on with each other, things might not be quite so bad.

Unfortunately, humanity's villainy frequently gets in the way, and over the course of a decade in the comic, human nature has been shown at its worst. Manipulative, greedy, murderous and downright evil, some truly bad people have featured. And just when you think they can't get any worse, the stakes will be upped in the even gorier next issue.

Perhaps it's not surprising that this world brings out the worst in people, and it would be a mistake to paint them all as simplistic horror villains. It's true some are more traditionally evil than others, but time and again, Robert Kirkman has thrown in twists and reversals, designed to confound the sympathies of the reader (Dwight is a good example). 'Heroes,' too, can be every bit as flawed and prone to behavior that, on the face of it, is... bad. Often you're left wondering, where does the hero stop and the villain begin?

GOING LOCO

Very few of the baddies of *The Walking Dead* would identify themselves as bad. Some are plain psychotic, and with the shackles of normal life removed, have let their most primal urges run free. Thomas Richards was a key early villain – not because he was in the comic for very long, but because he was the first human to show that a zombie plague does not automatically change human nature. He is an insane killer, who had been locked up for life; it is small wonder that the sudden arrival of men, women and children in the prison brings out Richards' barely suppressed murderous instincts. He couldn't care less that there are walkers roaming the world beyond the prison gates; he just wants to keep killing within the walls that he now calls home.

Similarly, the early signs of an emerging psychosis in Ben may have been accelerated by the unusual situation of the zombie apocalypse – especially traumatizing for a child – but they would have presumably occurred at some point anyway. His violent relationship with other children, the torture and killing of a cat, and finally the murder of his brother, Billy – the breakdown of society acts as a catalyst for these actions, but not necessarily a cause.

THOMAS RICHARDS COULDN'T CARE LESS THAT THERE ARE WALKERS ROAMING THE WORLD BEYOND THE PRISON GATES; HE JUST WANTS TO KEEP KILLING.

However, for many of the other villains, their behavior is justified by a desire to survive. Naturally, this takes many forms, and reveals the depths to which humanity will sink when the stakes are high. The Hunters cross a taboo utterly unacceptable in pre-apocalyptic society – cannibalism – and yet have no problem justifying it to Rick and his group.

"At the end of the day, no matter how much we may detest this ugly business, a man's gotta eat," Chris tells Dale, as they chow down on his remaining leg.

THE BIG BADS

Alpha, who led the Whisperers until recently, believes that for her group to survive in a walker-infested world, they must reduce themselves to the level of animal. Subjugation, rape, torture, murder – these are all justified actions if it means staying alive.

However, as her relationship with her daughter Lydia shows, she finds it difficult to surrender the final vestiges of humanity. She sends Lydia away to

THE HUNTERS CROSS A TABOO UTTERLY UNACCEPTABLE IN PRE-APOCALYPTIC SOCIETY – CANNIBALISM – AND YET HAVE NO PROBLEM JUSTIFYING IT.

live in Alexandria, rather than further subject her to the behavior she has sanctioned in others. Later on in the story, Alpha confesses how much she misses Lydia.

The two villains that cast the biggest shadow across *The Walking Dead* are the Governor and Negan. These are 'Big Bads', in the traditional dramatic sense – charismatic leaders that you love to hate, who know how to control their people with an uncompromising mix of ruthlessness, intelligence and charisma. And unlike some of the more simplistic bad guys, whose time in the comic is more fleeting, Kirkman keeps readers interested in them for many, many issues, leading to some fascinating places.

To the residents of Woodbury, the Govenor is a strong, fair, principled man. It's classic dictatorial manipulation; tell your people exactly what they want to hear, make it sound like everyone else beyond the walls are out to harm them, and you will inspire a following far more loyal and devoted than you would via fear and coercion. The Governor isn't above the latter either, but he reveals his true side only to his immediate subordinates, not the wider population of his community.

While there is no defending the deplorable treatment dished out to Rick and especially Michonne, the question remains – does the end justify the means? Until Rick and his group turn up at Woodbury, the Governor has managed to keep his people fed, clothed and relatively safe in an environment that doesn't exactly offer many of those things elsewhere. Does it matter that he cares more about power than he does about those he leads, if the end result is still the same, ie their safety? This is a different world.

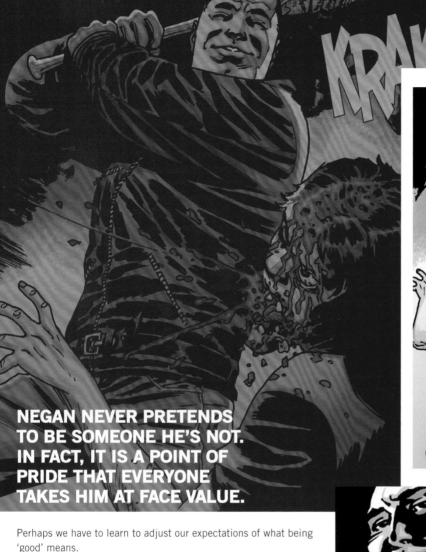

NEGAN NEVER PRETENDS TO BE SOMEONE HE'S NOT. IN FACT, IT IS A POINT OF PRIDE THAT EVERYONE TAKES HIM AT FACE VALUE.

HOLY SHIT-- HE'S TAKING IT LIKE A *CHAMP!*

Perhaps we have to learn to adjust our expectations of what being 'good' means.

An argument could be made that some of Rick's actions aren't exactly heroic. Perhaps he doesn't attempt to disguise the darker side of his nature from the group, but there's no question that Rick would do almost anything to protect his family, and those who trust in him to lead them. This is a man who bites out the throat of a bandit to protect Carl, and sanctions the brutal execution of the Hunters, butchering them and throwing their mutilated corpses into a fire as a show of strength. Understandable, perhaps even justified, but hardly the behavior of a 'civilized' man.

Rick was a lawman before the end of the world, which fools readers into thinking that he knows right from wrong, but we have to wonder how sympathetic Sheriff Rick would be to his post-apocalyptic self after looking at all the things he's done in-between. Not too kindly, we think.

THE BAT MAN
Negan, on the other hand, never pretends to be someone he's not. In fact, it is a point of pride that everyone takes him at face value. While the Governor, at first, appeared as a more ambiguous character, Negan's opening salvo is to smash out Glenn's brains in

THE GOVERNOR AND NEGAN ARE 'BIG BADS' IN THE TRADITIONAL DRAMATIC SENSE – CHARISMATIC LEADERS THAT YOU LOVE TO HATE.

front of his friends. His intent is clear right from the off. He is a more complex antagonist than the Governor, and indeed than any of the villainous characters in *The Walking Dead*, and we are still getting to know him after more than 50 issues.

Negan has become as important to the moral see-saw of *The Walking Dead* as Rick or any other 'hero.' At first, he just seemed to be a fouler mouthed variant on previous bad guys, but the slow reveal of a moral code – his view of rape is very different to that of the Governor's, for example – and his unwillingness to punish the weak unless it directly serves his cause, makes for a far more interesting character.

By the time we reach more recent issues, Negan is more an uneasy ally of Rick than an adversary. With the Whisperers now the main villains, an imprisoned Negan goes from advising Rick on how to deal with unrest among his men, to being released by Brandon, double-crossing him, infiltrating the Whisperers and then killing Alpha.

His final monologue to her, in which he describes himself as a "broken" man shows a vulnerability a world away from his initial appearance. Negan's development from cartoonish monster to complex, violent, yet very human individual is proof that concepts of villainy have evolved far beyond what would traditionally be found in genre fiction. May this evolution long continue. •

WHAT COMES AFTER

'Anatomy Of A Story' breaks down a specific *Walking Dead* tale into its component parts to analyze what makes it tick. With the release of the new 12-part comic story 'All Out War,' *TWDM* decided to bring you right up to date with an examination of Volume 18: 'What Comes After.' WORDS: Stuart Barr

Not unlike 'Here We Remain' (volume nine), 'What Comes After' has a difficult task. Both volumes follow bloody and dramatic story arcs that left characters (and readers) in shock. The immediate predecessor to Volume 18, 'Something to Fear,' may not quite approach the 'night of the long knives' of Volume Eight: 'Made to Suffer,' but it does

continues in the series to date. He miscalculated the strength of the Saviors, not realizing they could attack on two fronts. This cost Glenn his life.

He also seems oblivious to how expertly Negan judges character and, in particular, how effectively he exploits weakness. Glenn's execution left Rick looking broken and empty.

Outgunned by Negan's group, the Saviors, Rick has little choice but to accept the biker's terms of surrender. It's a bitter pill to swallow, especially as Negan is so diplomatic when taking the Alexandria Safe-Zone's supplies, telling Rick: "In case you haven't caught on, I just slid my dick down your throat and you thanked me for it."

However, Rick is nothing if not cunning. He wants to fool Negan into believing he has rolled over and showed his belly to the alpha dog. In order for this to be convincing, he needs the residents of the Alexandria Safe-Zone to also believe it, and so tells them to give up their supplies without fuss. It's a dangerous strategy, considering he's only recently assumed leadership and there are others waiting in the wings to usurp his position

> Negan's group has many aspects of a cult. There's blind faith in a leader, created and reinforced by systematic brutality.

include two of the most shocking and unexpected deaths in the entire saga, those of Sgt Abraham Ford and Glenn. The latter had been a part of the story since issue two, and Abraham was among the most capable characters to have been part of Rick's band. These deaths, and the manner of them, affect Rick and the other survivors deeply, and, as its title suggests, the repercussions (and recriminations) are dramatically felt in 'What Comes After.'

The first realization after the events of volume 17 is that Negan is both a charismatic and dangerous villain. Clearly a psychopath and borderline insane (then again, in this world, who isn't?), he is nevertheless smart and intuitive.

Rick underestimated Negan from the start, something that

(most notably Spencer Monroe, the son of the late Douglas Monroe, the former community leader). It is also a strategy that risks driving a wedge between him and his closest confidantes, even son Carl and lover Andrea.

For the reader, this is a frustrating time because Robert Kirkman only reveals the nature of Rick's plan drip by drip (a process that's still playing out as *TWDM* went to press). Frankly, it's hard to judge whether Rick has a detailed plan of attack; for the moment, it all seems rather scrappy and half-cocked.

The plan as it stands raises serious questions: does Rick really have the best interests of the group in mind here? Is he really just looking for revenge for the murder of his friend, Glenn? Is he prepared to risk his relationships and the lives of those around him to exact his plan? Is it morally right to effectively lie to the people caught in the crossfire? And finally, how capable is Rick as a leader given that Negan seems so readily able to manipulate him?

Rick does reveal some of his plan to Andrea when she threatens to move out of their home in disgust at his capitulation. However, he is unable to explain his stance to Carl, the repercussions of which will be felt later in this story. After releasing a captured Savior, the scarred Dwight, Rick has him followed by Paul 'Jesus' Monroe (unrelated to Douglas and Spencer) in the

hopes of finding Negan's base.

When Negan turns up at Alexandria's gate, Rick allows him to search houses and take valuable food and medical supplies. Unbeknown to him, a furious Carl steals Abraham's automatic rifle and hides in the Saviors' truck before it leaves for their base with the supplies. Upon arrival, Carl is discovered and kills several men before being subdued. Rather than kill him, Negan is amused and takes him under his wing, allowing us to see a little of the Saviors' base.

Negan's community is strict and brutal; members earn the right to stay within the walls. They must either join raiding parties, become guards or henchmen, or if female and deemed sufficiently attractive, they can join Negan's personal harem. There is one rule for Negan's concubines – they must never cheat on him. If any romantic dalliance is discovered, the woman either goes back to earning her place or gives up their lover. The man (often a former boyfriend or husband) is then horribly branded by the application of a red-hot iron to the face. As we discover, this is the source of Dwight's scars; one of Negan's concubines is revealed to be his wife.

Outgunned by the Saviors, Rick has little choice but to accept Negan's terms of surrender. It's a bitter pill to swallow.

OPPOSITE PAGE & THIS PAGE, LEFT & TOP LEFT: Negan takes stowaway Carl under his wing, despite Rick's son killing some of his army. THIS PAGE, ABOVE: Paul 'Jesus' Monroe knows how to kick walker butt with style.

IN A NUTSHELL

TITLE: What Comes After
FEATURED ISSUES: 103-108
COLLECTION: Volume 18
SYNOPSIS: Left devastated by the death of his friends, Glenn and Abraham, Rick capitulates to Negan's demands, telling the people of Alexandria that they are to hand over supplies in exchange for the protection of the Saviors. Andrea takes umbrage, so Rick reveals his duplicity, explaining that Negan will pay, but they need to bide their time. Upset with his father, Carl steals away in one of Negan's supply trucks and attempts to kill the Saviors' leader, only to be caught before he can do the deed. Rather than kill him, Negan shows Carl around the Saviors' camp before returning him to Alexandria, but not before inferring to Rick that his son has been butchered. This sends Rick into a rage, showing just how easily Negan gets under his skin. The story ends with Rick being introduced to King Ezekiel, leader of another survivors' camp, The Kingdom.

TIDBITS:

- This volume marks the introduction of Ezekiel, who seems to model his camp on Arthurian principles. His knights ride horses and carry lances. He also has a pet tiger, Shiva.

- Shiva is the name of one of the three main gods in Hinduism. The god is also known as The Destroyer and The Transformer. Fingers crossed Ezekiel's tiger is not a robot in disguise...

- The Alexandria Safe-Zone is now without supplies to treat serious medical conditions, with the Saviors taking all of the strong painkillers and narcotics, such as morphine and Oxycontin.

- Negan forces Carl to sing to his baseball bat, Lucille. Carl chooses popular folk song, 'You Are My Sunshine.' He's in good company – the song has been covered by the likes of Ray Charles, Johnny Cash and Celine Dion. It is also performed in the film *O Brother, Where Art Thou?* by The Soggy Bottom Boys.

Does Rick really have the best interests of the group in mind? Or is he just looking for revenge for the murder of his friend?

Negan's group has many aspects of a cult. Certainly there is blind faith in a leader created and reinforced by systematic brutality. The Saviors are essentially gangsters running a protection racket. Strong in numbers, well trained and armed, they are not self-sufficient so use their might to demand a 'tribute' from weaker communities in the Washington area. In exchange, they provide protection, but of course the only real protection on offer is from the very people the victims are paying to leave them alone.

Negan does eventually return Carl to Rick, but not before inciting him to violence by casually implying he has done something terrible to his son. This is a worrying event for everyone, or it least it would be if they knew Rick was trying to play a long game against the Saviors. Frankly, Rick is a terrible poker player, and Negan has got his number, correctly identifying Carl as his 'tell' and expertly exploiting it. In fact, Carl is unharmed but Negan's incitement of rage in

Rick, which results in a dust-up between the two, reveals just how much of an edge he has on Rick. As he says: "I'm a special kind of person. I don't fucking rattle."

The volume concludes with Paul telling Rick it's time he met Ezekiel. The pair travel to The Kingdom, another community in the area. Ezekiel is the leader, an imposing African-American with dreadlocks who styles himself as a 'King' and keeps a pet tiger (there's both more, and less, to this character but that's revealed in the next volume).

While the Saviors may seem like a cult, is The Kingdom any different? It may appear benign from its brief introduction, but it's just as cultish. Vaguely modeled on medieval chivalry, 'King' Ezekiel seems righteous, but one wonders if Rick is altogether too eager to find an ally in a man who walks around with a tiger on a lead. *TWDM* has a sneaky feeling there's a lot more to Ezekiel than meets the eye, and we're not entirely convinced he's trustworthy.

For now, they seem to want the same thing. Ezekiel wants to eliminate the Saviors, but has been

DOOM! DOOM!

Ezekiel seems righteous, but one wonders if Rick is altogether too eager to find an ally in a man who walks around with a tiger on a lead.

unwilling to move against them until the odds were in his favor. Two things have now changed: the battle-hardened nature of Rick's group and the arrival of Dwight, who is apparently willing to double-cross his master for the love of his woman.

Dualities are a common theme of *The Walking Dead*. Kirkman likes to set up protagonists and antagonists that are either in stark opposition or mirror each other. Despite being a ruthless psychopath, Negan actually has a code of honor. Scrupulously honest, there is little deceit in Negan's actions. When he makes a deal, he's not the one who breaks it; granted he has force and no small amount of intimidation on his side.

On the other hand, Rick is lying to almost everyone about the nature of his plans, and only the forthcoming story 'All Out War' will tell if less carnage, death and destruction would be wrought if the members of Alexandria had just paid Negan off.

What comes after? You'll just have to read on and find out... •

OPPOSITE PAGE, TOP: Negan may take a beating from Rick, but somehow still winds up on top. BOTTOM: Paul has proven to be a more than capable ally. THIS PAGE, TOP: Ezekiel has a tiger. LEFT: Is Dwight really someone to be trusted?

Scrupulously honest, there is little deceit in Negan's actions. Rick is the one who's lying.

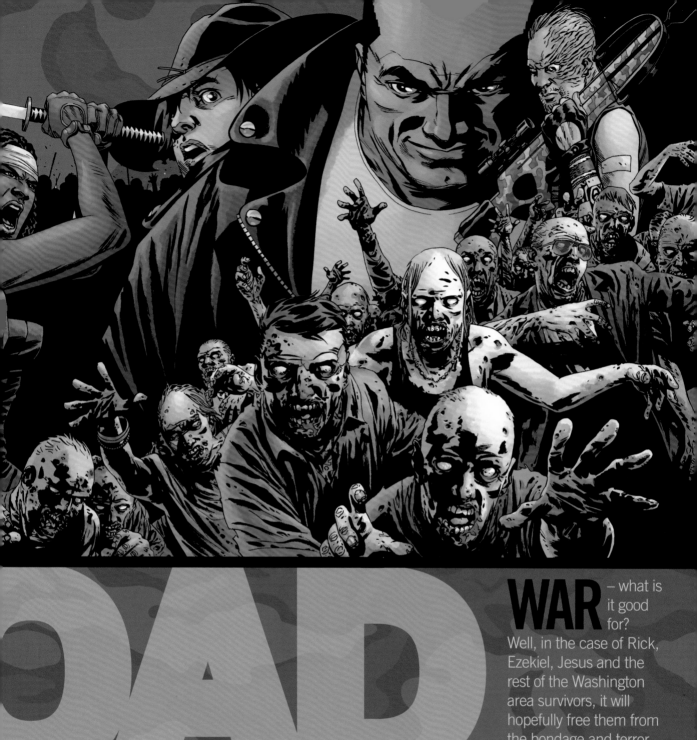

WAR

WAR – what is it good for? Well, in the case of Rick, Ezekiel, Jesus and the rest of the Washington area survivors, it will hopefully free them from the bondage and terror inflicted on them by Negan and the Saviors. With the battlelines firmly drawn in issue 115, the epic 12-part storyline 'All Out War' has been intensifying, with casualties mounting on both sides. Although the brutal murder of Glenn in issue 100 served as *The Walking Dead*'s own Austro-Hungarian Archduke assassination moment, as *TWDM* discovers, the machinations leading up to the conflict are much more complex. WORDS: Simon Williams

THE PRELUDE

Though the Saviors have been threatening and harassing the other local communities for some time, it was Rick's group who were the first to encounter the Saviors' leader, the murderous Negan. Before this moment in issue 100, Hilltop leader Gregory and his emissary Paul 'Jesus' Monroe admitted that they'd never actually met him, and had doubts as to whether he even existed at all.

In addition to maintaining a low profile, Negan has also gone to great lengths to ensure the location of his headquarters – the Sanctuary – has stayed a secret. So while the Saviors' brutality may have provoked enmity from the communities they have terrorized, any sort of meaningful strike against the group's base of operations was impossible previously. It's only thanks to Carl sneaking aboard Negan's vehicle, and Jesus's capture and subsequent escape, that the allies were able to get the intelligence they needed on the Saviors' location and formidable defenses, as well as useful insights into how the group functions.

THE SAVIORS

LEADER: Negan
HEADQUARTERS:
The Sanctuary, a former factory
DEFENSIVE CAPABILITIES:
Heavily fortified and surrounded by a chain-link fence, concrete barricades and impaled zombies
ESTIMATED FORCES: 60-100

With an obsession for being top dog, there have been times when Negan's overestimation of his own reputation has blinded him to the likelihood of retaliation from the communities he so casually brutalizes. There have been numerous situations where the Saviors' leader seems surprised when his group's ruthless methods have come back to bite him – though his insistence on armed back-up has saved him on more than one occasion.

Rick's (and Carl's) initial strategy was to target Negan himself, no doubt hoping that by cutting the head off the metaphorical Savior snake the body would wither and die. We can only speculate what would

"A CHAIN OF EVENTS WAS SET FORTH ON THIS DAY. A CHAIN OF EVENTS THAT COULD WELL LEAD TO THE DEATHS OF EVERY LAST ONE OF YOUR GROUP." NEGAN

happen to the Saviors if both Rick and Carl had succeeded and Negan had been successfully killed.

The Saviors seem to operate like a cult, with Negan treated by his followers as a kind of godlike figurehead. "Negan rules by fear," says Jesus in issue 114, "or by manipulating his people into believing he's the only thing keeping them alive. They worship him." So it is possible that with Negan dead, the Saviors would fall apart into the looser group of individual survivors they were before Negan brought them together.

Of course, it's also possible that a successor would step up and assume top dog of the

"WE'RE GOING TO WAR." NEGAN

group, though we can be sure this would not be without considerable bloodshed among the Saviors.

Negan has maintained his position through his brutality and seems content to rule his followers by fear. But as history has shown time and again, fear is not always the best motivator, especially when going up against someone who is truly respected, and even loved, such as Rick Grimes.

Negan's methods have already caused a schism in his own organization, for instance, with the apparent defection of Dwight, one of his top lieutenants. Might this eventually prove to be his undoing?

Rick's motivations for going up against Negan and the Saviors are multi-faceted. It started off as a way to trade with the Hilltop; without supplies of their own, Rick offered the only thing they did have – their muscle.

After Glenn's death and the Saviors' attack on Alexandria, it has become more personal. And although Rick acknowledged his mistake in seriously underestimating the Saviors the first time, he repeated this error when he called for the unprepared attack on Negan and his men as they were leaving Alexandria, not knowing that Negan had already established a larger back-up force in the surrounding area. It was only the timely intervention of Jesus and the arrival of Ezekiel and his group that saved Rick and the others from summary execution.

THE ALEXANDRIA SAFE-ZONE

LEADER: Rick Grimes, former cop   **HQ:** Alexandria Safe-Zone
DEFENSIVE CAPABILITIES: Walled community with isolated solar power grid (semi-functional) and working ammunition factory, surrounded by trenches and strategically placed cars   **ESTIMATED FORCES:** 20

Even if Rick's first encounter with Negan hadn't ended so violently and tragically, it's unlikely that he would ever have truly agreed to live in fealty to the Saviors like the Hilltop survivors. Rick has made it clear that he regards the Saviors' leader as far too unpredictable to ever be able to co-exist with. "We can't live by the whims of Negan," Rick says in issue 115. "We'd never survive. That psycho would be the death of us all."

THE HILLTOP

LEADERS: Gregory, Paul 'Jesus' Monroe
HQ: The Barrington House
DEFENSIVE CAPABILITIES:
Walled town with elevated location and working foundry (but no firearms)
ESTIMATED FORCES: 20

NO, I DON'T THINK YOU QUITE UNDERSTAND WHAT'S AT STAKE HERE.

THIS ALL FALLS APART WITHOUT YOU, RICK. ALL OF IT.

Though it would appear that, by offering to take on the Saviors in return for trade with the Hilltop, Rick is the key instigator of the war, it's actually Paul 'Jesus' Monroe who really sets events in motion.

Jesus tells Rick he approached the Alexandria Safe-Zone in order to facilitate an introduction to the Hilltop colony, ostensibly to establish trade links between the two groups. He had observed the Alexandria survivors for some time before making contact. Isn't it just as likely that Jesus was really on the look-out for a group with the potential to stand up to the Saviors? He certainly has the motivation, since it's the Hilltop – the largest community in the DC area – that has borne the brunt of Negan's group for so long.

This might explain why Jesus was so tolerant of the rough welcome he received at the hands of Rick and Michonne. Having spied on Rick and his group for a while, Jesus knew he'd found the perfect allies for the war he (and Ezekiel) were eager for, and he clearly felt it was worth enduring several quite brutal beatings, and even imprisonment, if it meant he could get Rick and the rest on his side.

But Jesus was sincere when he told Rick he believed the former cop was building something better. "When you're done," he says, "the world will be changed. Renewed. Better. I want to be a part of that. I want to do whatever I can to help make that a reality."

> **"YOU GIVE PEOPLE COURAGE, YOU INSPIRE PEOPLE TO STAND UP... TO FIGHT FOR WHAT'S RIGHT... YOU'RE A LEADER WE CAN FOLLOW." JESUS TO RICK**

THE KINGDOM

LEADER: Ezekiel, former zookeeper
HQ: Former high school
DEFENSIVE CAPABILITIES: Wall consisting of sheet metal and school buses, guarded by armored 'knights' on horseback
ESTIMATED FORCES: 30 (plus Shiva the tiger)

Ezekiel, the leader of the Kingdom, has been waiting for some time for an opportunity to strike back against the "tyrant" Negan and his Saviors. But he's still an unknown quantity from Jesus' point of view, and had not made his opinion of Negan fully known before the arrival of Rick (though having seen Negan's methods, it's understandable).

We don't know exactly why Ezekiel hates Negan so much. Perhaps it's simply because of the vicious way Negan and his group extort supplies from the neighboring communities, or there may be a more personal history between the two that has yet to be revealed.

> **"THIS PLACE IS SPECTACULAR... VERY MUCH WORTH FIGHTING FOR." EZEKIEL**

> ## "WHATEVER COMES OF THIS. WHATEVER IT TAKES. IT'LL BE WORTH IT."
> ### ANDREA

THE BREAKING POINT

Despite a gradual escalation of violence between Rick's group and the Saviors, which included several killings and attempted killings, the eventual immediate trigger for the war was as unpredictable as Negan himself.

In fairness to the Saviors' leader, he was willing to forgive a number of serious provocations. But the breaking point came soon after Rick's rather reckless attempt on Negan's life, when Carl shot a chunk out of Lucille, the Savior leader's beloved baseball bat and, according to Negan himself, the only woman he has ever truly loved. Coming from anyone else, this might sound insincere, but from Negan, you can believe it!

When the Alexandria survivors inside the Safe-Zone refused to give up Carl, Negan prepared to bludgeon to death Nicolas, Holly and Heath in turn until they did. It was only the arrival of Jesus and Ezekiel and his group (particularly Shiva) on the scene that prevented a massacre outside the gates to the Safe-Zone and caused a rout that sent Negan and his group fleeing to the hills.

While Rick was keen to press forward while they had the advantage of surprise, calmer heads prevailed. "We were not prepared for this," Ezekiel says, happier to let the Saviors retreat. "Let them run before they realize they still outnumber us."

But it didn't take them long to prepare, and with Carl and Andrea left in charge of the Safe-Zone's defenses, Rick's meager forces, bolstered with those of the Kingdom and Hilltop, have a plan to take the fight to Negan with a full frontal attack on the Sanctuary itself.

THE REAL ENEMY

It has not gone unnoticed, as the series has progressed, that the threat posed by zombies has been relegated and largely superseded by that of other living survivors. There hasn't been a single character death directly attributable to a zombie since issue 83, when Douglas Monroe, Jessie Anderson and her son Ron were killed by roamers which broke into Alexandria. Though their deaths were tragic, the way the community rallied round to drive the walkers back made

manageable threat. And from that point on, the series has reflected this, dialing down the danger posed by the dead and focusing

It's perhaps appropriate that, of all the survivors, it's Negan who realizes the true threat. In issue 112, when Rick unwisely taunts the Saviors' leader for bringing a baseball bat to a gun fight, Negan's hidden back-up snipers quickly prove Rick wrong, shooting Rick's pistol right out of his hand.

Negan calmly explains to Rick that they merely use their blunt instruments for the dead, and save the bullets for "the much more dangerous, but slightly less

ALL OUT WAR, PART ONE

'All Out War' is one of the comic series' best storylines, packed with action, great character arcs, moments of self-sacrifice, and some thrilling encounters, as Rick leads the combined forces of Alexandria, the Hilltop and the Kingdom against Negan and the Saviors. *TWDM* examines the events of the first part, as the war escalates between the two forces. WORDS: Stuart Barr

A major factor in the continuing success of *The Walking Dead* is Robert Kirkman's skill at balancing character and action. As fans, we remember the big moments (the Governor's prison siege, the herd overrunning Alexandria, issue 100), but the characters keep us coming back, whether we love them or, indeed, love to hate them.

Volume 20 begins an ambitious 'event' storyline. Since the arrival of Negan and the Saviors, tensions and violence have escalated. In the previous volume, 'March To War,' Rick Grimes

In order to win the war, Rick must be prepared for his people to lay down their lives. [But] he is not yet ready to do this.

saw an opportunity to deal with the threat once and for all. With Paul 'Jesus' Monroe acting as an intermediary, he has persuaded the communities of Alexandria, Hilltop, and the Kingdom to form an alliance.

Negan is not an insane despot like the Governor, but someone far more focused, better equipped and altogether more daunting an opponent.

In the action-packed first half of the 'All Out War' arc, Rick takes the initiative, marching a ragtag army to the fences of Negan's safe-zone, the Sanctuary. He audaciously demands Negan to surrender, promising non-combative Saviors will be spared. Negan declines, using a mixture of harsh language and lead.

Ram-Packed Action

Despite a Savior sniper scoring first blood, Rick's forces turn the tide of battle, deliberately creating a cacophony that attracts walkers. Rick intends to ram a bus through the gates, gambling that Negan will want him alive, but in a selfless act, the late Abraham's partner, Holly, forcibly commandeers the vehicle. The

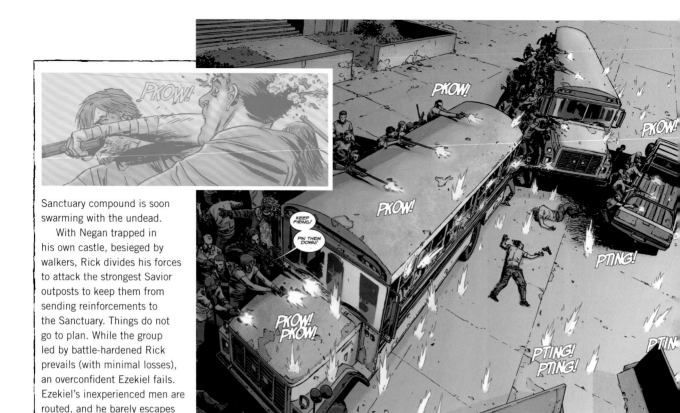

Sanctuary compound is soon swarming with the undead.

With Negan trapped in his own castle, besieged by walkers, Rick divides his forces to attack the strongest Savior outposts to keep them from sending reinforcements to the Sanctuary. Things do not go to plan. While the group led by battle-hardened Rick prevails (with minimal losses), an overconfident Ezekiel fails. Ezekiel's inexperienced men are routed, and he barely escapes with his life.

Having returned to Alexandria, Rick is dismayed to hear of Ezekiel's failure and calls an urgent meeting, knowing that with reinforcements to quell the walker incursion, Negan will soon move against Alexandria. Negan arrives before the defenses can be properly organized, and the Saviors cause panic by lobbing grenades over the walls. Only the timely arrival of Maggie and some of Hilltop's residents prevents total disaster.

"Freedom!"

What makes Volume 20 so satisfying is that, while this plot synopsis demonstrates how much can be packed into six issues, Kirkman still finds time to include important character beats, memorable dialogue, and develop themes woven through the comic's fabric since Rick discovered the other communities in the Washington area.

By this point in the story, Rick is psychologically in a strong place. He has survived a mental breakdown in the wake of his wife and baby daughter's deaths; he has survived seeing good friends die; he has survived even the near death of his son. Initial skirmishes with Negan may have gone badly because Rick underestimated his foe, but now he has a better understanding of Negan, who is not an insane despot like the Governor, but someone far more focused, better equipped and altogether more daunting as an opponent.

Rick wants to be a wartime general – his opening attack on the Sanctuary is well planned, his *Braveheart*-esque speech to the troops is stirring, his ultimatum to Negan is intimidating. Yet, in

one area, he is still not fully committed to the role of leader. In the deceptively quiet and intimate opening of issue 115, Rick tells Andrea with regret that they can't have a war without casualties. Andrea's reply is blunt: "Then we have been at war since the beginning."

Leadership Woes

In order to win the war, Rick must be prepared for his people to lay down their lives. It is apparent in the preliminary battle, he is not

ready to do this. The plan to drive a bus into Negan's compound is sound. Rick's insistence on doing this himself is borderline idiotic. Without leadership the war will fail, and there are few other candidates capable of leading his army as effectively.

What Rick has not realized is that even if he is not yet willing to ask for sacrifice, those he leads are already inclined to step up. Holly decides to take the choice away from him, commandeering the bus. Later, in the chaos of Negan's grenade attack on Alexandria, Denise makes a decision to sacrifice her life. She has received a walker bite on her arm, amputation could conceivably save her, but she needs both arms in order to save the wounded.

It could be argued that neither Holly nor Denise are motivated primarily by loyalty to Rick. Holly wants revenge for the murder of Abraham Ford by the Saviors. Denise, meanwhile, wants to save Heath. However, Rick has created a community and an idea of freedom that people are willing to die for. His arc in this volume is all about Rick coming to recognize this.

Rick is not the only 'king' on the chessboard though. His strengths are further demonstrated in contrast to Gregory and Ezekiel. Gregory is weak: he has no qualms about asking others to die for him if it will save his own skin. When Rick confronts Negan at the Sanctuary, Gregory is produced, announcing he stands with the Saviors. To Negan's rage, this only leads to eight men from Hilltop vacating the battle.

Ezekiel is more firmly on Rick's side, but his problem is that he is a demagogue. He leads by showing his people an impressive public image (replete with tiger), but when pushed into a corner this image cracks, revealing his critical inexperience. Michonne skewers his weakness ruthlessly after his failed outpost attack:

Ezekiel is a demagogue. He leads by showing his people an impressive public image, but when pushed into a corner, this image cracks.

"If you're really this much of a pussy, do what you do best... Act like you aren't."

The strongest leader among Rick's allies emerges unexpectedly when circumstances make Maggie Greene step up. Gregory returns to Hilltop after being pushed off a roof by Negan. He

Gregory is weak: he has no qualms about asking others to die for him if it will save his own skin.

begins agitating against Rick, advising residents to bow to Savior demands. Disgusted, Maggie punches him in the face and confronts the Hilltop people with her reading of the situation. Gregory originally asked Rick to take out Negan, and this is exactly what he is doing. If they capitulate to Negan, they will be beholden to him forever. Maggie ends her speech: "I believe in Rick Grimes."

All Hail Negan!

Then there is Negan himself, the great dictator. He leads through fear and manipulation, but his methods are undeniably effective. His army marches to his tune because he gives them security. Under attack, he exposes no weakness.

Negan is also quick to adapt and take advantage of events. When Holly is captured, she is initially mistaken for Andrea.

When she convinces him otherwise, he moves on to more pressing matters (such as the walkers that have overrun the Sanctuary). Then something interesting happens. Negan returns to find Holly about to be sexually assaulted by one of his own men. This enrages him and he kills the man, declaring: "We don't rape." Is this a genuine rule? It seems to be. Negan has his harem, but maintains a pretense that this is consensual. He is also an arch-manipulator. Given that his rule is predicated on offering security alongside a strict 'rule of law,' perhaps this is just a pretense?

Negan's skill at exploiting weakness is later demonstrated when he offers a hooded and bound Holly to Rick at the Alexandria gates as an olive branch before initiating talks. Rick should know that Negan would not be so understanding. He makes a serious tactical error in trusting him, and a bound and hooded Walker Holly stumbles blindly towards the voices of the Alexandrians

calling her. When the hood is removed, the undead Holly bites Denise. With his opponents thrown off-guard, Negan attacks, creating chaos. His 'Trojan Holly' is an act of calculated cruelty, but it gives the Saviors an edge.

Negan is a classic pop-culture psychopath. Charming, poetic (albeit with a 'bawdy' turn of phrase), intelligent, manipulative, lacking empathy. Nevertheless, he is also calculating and organized. When his attack on Alexandria is going well, he appears to be sexually aroused. Or perhaps even more disturbingly, he feigns this as an intimidation tactic. It certainly serves to keep his lieutenants on edge.

Negan's disadvantage is that because he seems to see his people only as tools, he is never going to inspire true loyalty. This is most obvious with Dwight. He should be a trusted advisor, but Negan has pushed him into formenting rebellion.

Facing Death

Alongside leadership, another theme arises in this volume for almost all characters. This is a sense of mortality, the fear of loss, and its effect on their actions. For Rick it is the motivator – everything he does is to protect those closest to him. Carl shows signs of becoming a future

> ## The end score is Rick two, Negan two, but it is most definitely advantage Negan.

leader, but he is equally concerned about his father, however hard he does not want to show it. When Eric is killed in Rick's outpost attack, Aaron becomes consumed with revenge. When Rick asks if he will be OK, he responds: "Not until every one of [the Saviors] is dead." Michonne has become intimate with Ezekiel, she won't call it a 'relationship' but acknowledges it might become one. This is a big step for her. Most movingly, Denise forgoes the amputation that could save her life to save others, namely her friend, Heath.

Hilltop is now split between Gregory's loyalists and Maggie's splinter group. Will Gregory have a role to play in part two? Ezekiel's spirit seems broken. Can he recover, and without Shiva by his side, has his carefully manufactured image faded too much to inspire loyalty?

Maggie's support could not be more opportune for Rick. He also has Dwight in the enemy camp. Negan may not be aware of Eugene Porter's success at manufacturing bullets.

Part one of 'All Out War' ends with Negan pushed back, but Alexandria in flames. As a numbers game, it appears to be a draw. Rick has won two early victories, but Savior forces defeated Ezekiel and have devastated Alexandria. The end score is Rick two, Negan two, but it is most definitely advantage Negan.

Game on! •

IN A NUTSHELL

TITLE: 'All Out War, Part One'
FEATURED ISSUES:
#115 to 120
COLLECTION: Volume 20
SYNOPSIS: Leading the combined forces of Alexandria, Hilltop and the Kingdom against Negan and his Saviors, Rick believes he has the might to defeat him and offers him a one-time chance to surrender. Negan has far too much of an ego to simply roll over, however, and the war starts.

The first battle at the Sanctuary goes in Rick's favor, but the tide turns when the Saviors defeat Rick's troops at other Savior compounds and then mount a counter-attack against Alexandria. Both sides suffer losses, including the deaths of Holly, Denise, and Ezekiel's tiger, Shiva. By part one's close, the war is evenly balanced and the story is poised for round three.

TIDBITS:

• 'All Out War' is the first story arc in the comic's history to be split over two volumes (12 issues). The frequency of release was also changed, with issues released every two weeks, rather than every month.

• In order to keep up with the increased frequency, artist Dave Stewart and inker Stefano Gaudiano were brought onboard to help out regular series artist Charlie Adlard. Stewart created the colored cover art for all 12 issues, while Gaudiano inked the interiors, leaving Adlard to illustrate the internal panels. A special hardback 'Artist Proof' edition of 'All Out War,' containing all 12 issues, was released which showcases Adlard's original pencils.

• You can read exclusive interviews with Gaudiano and Stewart, where they talk about their *Walking Dead* experiences, in issues 7 and 8 of *TWDM* respectively.

TOP 5
DEATH BECOMES THEM
Top Five Sacrifices for the Common Good

AXEL ROSE

Always passive and seemingly never fazed, former biker Axel will be remembered for helping the survivors set up defenses at the prison in what turned out to be a wasted effort to fight off the Governor's malevolent advances. He also stood up for our group when the other prisoners, under the leadership of Dexter, tried to oust them.

Axel's last stand was in the final battle for the prison. He died trying to protect the group, shot by a Woodbury

soldier. Even in the face of imminent death he didn't seem stressed, announcing calmly, that he and the gang were "fucked." ◇◇◇◇◇◇

WHUMP!

BLAM!

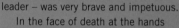

DON'T LET HIM IN! **DON'T--**

CHOP-CHOP!

4. Despite their ups and downs and disagreements, Tyreese was Rick's second-in-command for a long time. His capture by the Governor's men – he and Michonne chased after them after their first assault on the prison in the hopes of killing their leader – was very brave and impetuous.

In the face of death at the hands of the Governor, Tyreese pleaded with the group to not give up the prison in exchange for his life. At the time it was an honorable gesture, but, as is often the case with *The Walking Dead*, his act of defiance only delayed the result – and resulted in him losing his head. Nevertheless, his sacrifice was profound, and gave the group time to plan a defense. ◇◇

TAINTED MEAT

3. Dale's death wasn't a sacrifice but he was always a character willing to put the common good ahead of himself.

When Rick couldn't handle the pressures of the prison, he stepped up as *de facto* leader, providing wisdom and advice to the younger members of the group. His death was slow, painful and drawn out, but it did galvanize the group into a stoic mentality, which they still have to this day.

After getting bitten by a walker, Dale's first instinct was to protect the emotions of others – Andrea, in particular. He hid his wound to spare her the pain and left the safety of Gabriel's church to die away from the others. However, he was caught by the Hunters, who proceeded to eat half of his leg. At least he had the final laugh… ◇◇◇◇◇

I'M TAINTED MEAT!

YOU'RE EATING TAINTED MEAT!

TAINTED MEAT!

2. FROM ZERO TO HERO

Nicholas' last act was one of true sacrifice: stepping in to save our main man, Rick, and taking a knife slash across his back from a Savior. What no one knew at the time was the knife had been coated in walker blood, meaning his chance of surviving the wound was zero. Despite initially having seen Rick as a problem and being a real thorn in our hero's side (even trying to oust him from Alexandria at one point), Nicholas eventually realized Rick was the right man to lead Alexandria. He came over to the good guys and stood shoulder-to-shoulder with them as they stood up to the advances of Negan and the Saviors. Sadly for him, his surviving wife and their child, his heroics led to a rather painful death. ◇◇◇◇◇◇◇◇◇◇◇◇

1. LOYAL TO THE END

Richard was a loyal servant to King Ezekiel, the lead protector of The Kingdom. In turn, that meant he was a vital ally to Rick and the gang. During the build-up to the events in 'All Out War,' he familiarized himself with the group and showed himself to be a key part in the plans to invade Negan's Sanctuary.

During its invasion, he became the victim of a gunshot to the chest and subsequently died in the arms of his leader. His death, like many of the other unknown lives lost in the war with Negan, was the biggest sacrifice simply because it helped Rick's assembled forces eventually rid themselves of the scourge of the Saviors. As the chief 'marine' of The Kingdom, all we have to say is *semper fi*, Richard, *semper fi*! ◇◇

DWIGHT

Dwight is one of the most compelling characters in *The Walking Dead*. At first, he's an individual, responsible for some terrible deeds that affect Rick and his group. Then he's an undercover ally of Rick's, maybe not a trusted one but certainly no friend of Negan. Then he's a community leader. Then he renounces leadership to fight the good fight out in the field. Like a chameleon changing its color to match its different surroundings, Dwight's allegiances seem as permutable as they come. WORDS: Stuart Barr

feelings. But, in true *The Walking Dead* style, it is brutally truncated mid-sentence when he is struck on the back of the head with a crossbow bolt.

The fatal shot was made by Dwight. Acting as an emissary for the Saviors, Dwight cuts an intimidating figure. He's foul-mouthed (like his boss), and has terrible Freddie Krueger-esque burns covering half his face and head. In the previous issue, a party led by Rick Grimes encountered the Saviors for the first time; the meeting did not go too well for them. Dwight is leading the second party, and is hellbent on impressing upon the residents of Alexandria that the Saviors mean business. Dwight apologizes to Eugene for killing his companion with zero sincerity. "This isn't how we like to start a new business arrangement," he says. Yeah, right!

FIRST APPEARANCE

Dwight swaggered onto *The Walking Dead* stage in issue 98, part of the 'Something To Fear' storyline that introduced the Saviors.

Returning to Alexandria, Abraham Ford and Eugene Porter are sharing a moment of 'bromance' following a fraught period in their relationship. Eugene receives Abraham's blessing to move forward with a relationship with Rosita. It is touching to see such a towering hunk of machismo as Abraham admitting his

"I'LL BRING YOU THAT ASSHOLE'S HEAD ON A SILVER PLATTER... AND THIS NIGHTMARE WILL, AT LONG LAST, BE OVER."

WORST MOMENT

Dwight's worst moment comes shortly after his introduction. After killing Abraham, he takes Eugene hostage. His Savior group approaches the gates of Alexandria, forcing Eugene to his knees before the crossbow-wielding Dwight. Facing Rick, Dwight demands entry to the community and the right to "take whatever, or whoever we want." This tough talking is brought to an abrupt and painful end when Eugene suddenly sinks

his teeth into Dwight's crotch with the force and tenacity of a pit bull chomping on a new chew toy. It is arguable which is worse to Dwight, the pain or the humiliation – we're kidding, it's most definitely the pain. Much later, when Eugene is again captured by the Saviors, he will remind Dwight of this moment by sneering that as long as he isn't gagged he is "still dangerous."

DWIGHT THE SOLDIER

Little is known about Dwight's life before the walker apocalypse, but from the start we can deduce that he was a hunter from his skill with a crossbow and ability to set an ambush. Later, there are references to a military career. This is carried over into the post-apocalypse world and his life with the Saviors. Wiry and lean, Dwight is not the most physically imposing member of Negan's gang. However, he has a tactical proficiency and an understanding of weapons that make him valuable to Negan despite their relationship being extremely prickly.

> BREAK RANKS! WE'RE SURROUNDED!

> FORM A CIRCLE, WORK YOUR WAY FORWARD, AWAY FROM EACH OTHER... GIVE US AN AREA TO RETREAT TO IF NEEDED!

> MOVE!

> SHUT UP, BITCH.

DWIGHT'S ROMANCES

Dwight got married before the fall of civilization and his wife, Sherry, is also a member of the Saviors. However, Sherry has chosen to become one of Negan's 'wives,' leaving Dwight's wife as the top dog's concubine. Sherry chose this to ensure that her and Dwight's lives are made easier; Negan's wives are granted special privileges. This comes at a price. Negan demands monogamy from his harem.

Missing each other, Dwight and Sherry attempt to have an affair but are discovered by Negan, who makes an example of Dwight by burning his face with a hot iron. Negan marks any man

"I'M NOT TRYING TO SAY I'M A GOOD MAN, OR THAT I REGRET ANYTHING I'VE DONE OR THAT I'VE CHANGED. I'M SAYING I WANT WHAT YOU WANT... RIGHT NOW."

who sleeps with his wives in this way – an ironic version of the Puritan scarlet letter.

When Sherry resumes her life as a wife of Negan, and even becomes a kind of den mother to the new initiates of the harem, Dwight's love for her turns to a mixture of hate and shame. This is something Negan is keenly aware of and naturally uses to humiliate Dwight in front of the other Saviors.

NOT ONE WORD TO NEGAN ABOUT *ANY* OF THIS. NOT ONE DAMN WORD.

AGREED.

BAD LIEUTENANT

With his strategic skills, Dwight is Negan's chief lieutenant. Negan depends on Dwight to enforce his will over the various settlements from which the group plunder supplies. Negan knows Dwight hates him, and Dwight is keenly aware that Negan will only tolerate his continued existence if he is useful.

THERE'S ALWAYS A NEXT TIME, I SUPPOSE.

I GET THAT I'M PROBABLY THE SECOND TO LAST PERSON YOU'D EVER WANT TO SEE, BUT YOU NEED TO UNDERSTAND SOMETHING.

IT APPEARS I'VE HAD A CHANGE OF HEART, BUT I ASSURE YOU, I'VE NEVER BEEN FULLY IN SUPPORT OF NEGAN.

After Negan kills Glenn in issue 100, Dwight is briefly captured by the Alexandrians. The community wishes to execute him, but Rick decides to release him, asking Jesus to track Dwight and discover the location of the Savior's home base: The Sanctuary. Tables flip again and Dwight captures Jesus. This may have been part of the plan all along, because Jesus then escapes just as they arrive at the stronghold. Knowing Negan will be less than charitable, Dwight demands the group says nothing of Jesus' escape.

When Negan humiliates Dwight once too often, expressing his 'ownership' of Sherry in graphic language after a game of ping pong, Dwight turns up in the Kingdom just as Jesus introduces Rick to Ezekiel for the first time. Dwight proposes to work with them to undermine Negan from inside the Saviors. To say Rick is extremely dubious is putting it mildly, but Dwight becomes a key and decisive figure in the coming battle to overthrow Negan.

SURE, WHATEVER.

I TAKE IT RICK DIDN'T FILL YOU IN, BUT I WANT NEGAN DEAD MORE THAN *ANY* OF YOU. I'M DOING EVERYTHING I CAN ON THE INSIDE TO HELP OUT.

SO DON'T TRY ANYTHING STUPID AND GET YOURSELF KILLED. I THINK I CAN GET YOU AND THE OTHERS OUT OF HERE.

A SERVANT OF TWO MASTERS

During the 'All Out War' storyline, Dwight's loyalties are somewhat fluid. Now acting as a double agent, but still in a position of seniority among the Saviors, he is placed in some very tough situations.

In retaliation for a strike against the Sanctuary, Negan has Dwight lead an attack against Alexandria armed with grenades. Dwight's military training is again hinted at when he instructs his men on how to "cook" grenades with knowledge clearly more in-depth than could be gained by playing a lot of *Call Of Duty*.

After Dwight abdicates as the Savior leader, he travels to Alexandria and arrives just as Rick is forming a militia to tackle the Whisperer threat.

He carries Negan's barbed wire-wrapped baseball bat, Lucille, into battle. When asked why he has kept the weapon as a method of execution, given its grisly history, he replies: "This bat represents a lot to me... oppression, misery... authority. I feel like it's my responsibility to change that."

"THIS BAT REPRESENTS A LOT TO ME... OPPRESSION, MISERY... AUTHORITY. I FEEL LIKE IT'S MY RESPONSIBILITY TO CHANGE THAT."

It's clear that Dwight is altering his strategy on the fly and playing the odds during this battle, illustrated when he makes a split-second decision not to press on with the attack on Alexandria, and instead turns his gun on his own men. He persuades the Safe-Zone, and more importantly Rick, to trust him by turning over the remaining grenades.

When Negan leads his forces in an assault on Hilltop, Dwight is at his side. Negan has him poison his crossbow bolts by dipping them in walker blood. Given the opportunity to hit Rick, he is forced to shoot by Negan. The resulting wound isn't instantly mortal but the bacteria should do the deed. However, unbeknown to Negan, Dwight has used a clean bolt and deliberately avoided a kill-shot. Later, when Rick faces off against Negan in hand-to-hand combat, Dwight stops other Saviors from coming to their leader's aid. The confrontation is decisive, and as such, Dwight plays a pivotal role in Negan's fall.

"STAY BACK. LET THEM FIGHT IT OUT."

DWIGHT FACT FILE

NAME: Dwight
AKA: 'D' (in TV series)
PLAYED ON TV BY: Austin Amelio
APPROX. AGE: Early 30s
JOB: Unknown, but possibly a soldier (pre-apocalypse); Negan's lieutenant, Savior leader, Militia member (post-apocalypse)
RELATIONSHIPS PRE-APOCALYPSE: Sherry (wife – comic); Honey (wife – TV); Tina (sister-in-law – TV)
RELATIONSHIPS POST-APOCALYPSE: Laura
LIKES: Crossbows, Sherry, Laura
DISLIKES: Negan, Sherry, Lucille
FIRST APPEARANCE: Issue 98; Season six, episode six – 'Always Accountable'
CURRENT STATUS: Alive

UNEASY LIES THE HEAD

Somewhere in the two-year time jump that follows 'All Out War,' Dwight becomes leader of the Saviors, initiates trade with the communities they formerly plundered, reunites with Sherry, and then loses her. We discover all this when Dwight meets Rick after a long time and the two have a heart-to-heart catch-up. Dwight expresses his doubt over his former foe and reveals he no longer wants to lead the Saviors.

When Dwight discovers Alexandria is being threatened by the Whisperers, he makes his break with the Saviors and returns to the Safe-Zone with Negan's fearsome personal weapon, the baseball bat he calls Lucille.

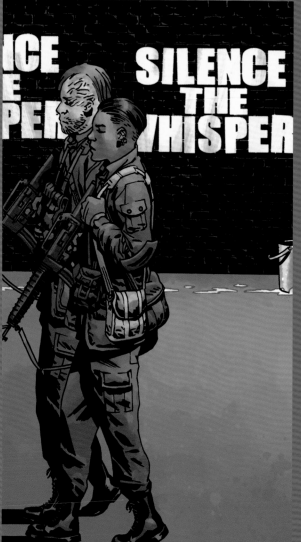

REDEMPTION SONG

In volunteering for Rick's militia, Dwight returns to his former life as a soldier. He is most at home as a squad leader. Dwight has tried living the life of the officer classes and moving away from the frontline to be a general, but he is happiest in the trenches. The journey of this character covers a lot of ground, beginning as a hated villain and the cold-blooded killer of a beloved character. But he ends up as a staunch ally of Rick and a fearsome warrior in defence of its freedom.

The Walking Dead fundamentally changed when Rick's group were taken into Alexandria by Aaron back in issue 68. Gradually, this nomadic group realized that they had found a place to build a real community and then a wider world beyond, opening up trade routes and diplomacy. They finally stopped running and created a sustainable society (the prison was a refuge, not a home).

"WE DON'T HAVE TO BE AFRAID OF [NEGAN] OR HIS RULES ANYMORE. THINGS WILL BE BETTER NOW. YOU'LL SEE."

This necessitated a change in, or at least a development of, their morality. In war, the lines are quite clear, but following the defeat of Negan, the communities of Alexandria, Hilltop, the Kingdom and the Sanctuary move into peaceful coexistence. In order for this to work, former enemies must become allies and this means that past transgressions on all sides must be forgiven and reconciled. Dwight embodies this.

Bringing the character right up to date, Dwight seems to have found a measure of peace, even a new love with an equally uncompromising former Savior Laura, who stands by him and follows him to the Safe-Zone where she also joins Rick's militia.

DEATH SENTENCE

Remember that character who was doomed as soon as they stepped into frame? No? Our 'Death Sentence' feature is here to help. Meet Doug.

WORDS: Dan Auty

THE CONDEMNED

Doug was one of the post-time jump Hilltop guards, responsible for keeping the residents safe from walkers. We first meet him when he is dispatched alongside Dante and another unnamed guard to find Ken, who went missing while on a routine patrol. Seems like a nice guy; time for him to die.

ALL IN A DAY'S WORK

Doug only graces the pages of *The Walking Dead* for a couple of issues, and while he faces a dangerous predicament in issue 131 – coming up against a large group of walkers alongside his two colleagues – it's seemingly nothing that these trained survivors aren't equipped to deal with. If they have made it this far, they know how to stay alive, right?

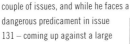

CHOP CHOP!

As issue 132 starts, it doesn't seem like Doug has much to worry about. Despite the waves of undead advancing upon

the trio, they clearly know exactly what to do, chopping heads and smashing brains in with a controlled, unpanicked efficiency. But hold on – are those walkers talking? And carrying knives? Uh-oh!

NICE KNOWING YA!

This is one of the first encounters with the Whisperers. At this point, our poor heroes have no idea that they are actually facing murderous humans clad in zombie skin, but they do know that these walkers are fighting back and it's time to run. Unfortunately for Doug, a knife in the back ensures that he's going nowhere; another through his neck seals the deal. Bye-bye Doug! •

THE SECRET DIARY OF A WALKER

It's not easy being a zombie in *The Walking Dead* world, as our week in the life/death of an undead walker shows. Diary entries transcribed by Dan Auty…

MONDAY

Bad start to a bad week! Daisy-Lou forgot her house keys again, and had to come down to the factory to get mine. I keep pointing out that no one's gonna be trying to steal nothing from our place, but she says you can't be too careful.

TUESDAY

Daisy-Lou here. Buck is at work so asked me to fill in this stupid diary for him. That damn fool is always leaving the doors to our house open. Has he seen some of the folk round here? Ugly, slobbering, stinking losers. And that's just our kids!

WEDNESDAY

Daisy-Lou reckons there are some normos here. She didn't want me going out in case we ran into them, but I thought it might be good to eat, er, see some fresh faces.

THURSDAY

Daisy-Lou again. Buck thinks he's so smart leaving the door open the whole time. And what do you know… we now got some damn normos living in our house! Some bratty kid and a bearded weirdo with one hand have holed up in our house. They rolled up last night while we were out. And then they locked the damn door behind them! I don't know who I'm more mad at!

FRIDAY

Man, Daisy-Lou is pissed at me! Those normos are still in there, and they ain't coming out. We tried banging on the front door, then peering through the windows at the back. The beardy freak has been sleeping all day. Lazy! This is why this country is in the state it's in. •

ALL OUT WAR, PART TWO

The war for control of the Washington area intensifies as the troops from Alexandria, Hilltop and The Kingdom face off against the vast numbers of the Saviors. Who will win between Rick and Negan? As Connor MacCleod of the Clan MacCleod once said, there can be only one.

WORDS: Stuart Barr

There is plenty of incident in 'All Out War, Part Two,' but in comparison to the first part, with its large scale battles, here, it is the clash between Rick Grimes and Negan that is foregrounded. Other players take subordinate roles, or, in the case of former Hilltop leader, Gregory, don't register in the storyline at all.

Part one ended with Negan pressing his attack on Alexandria, only to then be forced back by the sudden arrival of the Hilltop cavalry, led by Maggie. The situation continues to deteriorate, however. Eugene Porter and his team are captured when Saviors stumble across their munitions factory. Elsewhere, a demoralized Ezekiel is preparing to pull his men out of the war, following the deaths of Richard and Shiva. And Alexandria is too damaged by Negan's last attack to be effectively defended.

> Rick leaves behind the phone he used to talk to his dead wife. It's a clear sign he's finally healed from the psychological wounds caused by the death of Lori.

Rick takes the decision to move his people to Hilltop, but before leaving, there are consequences to deal with. Denise is dying of a walker bite. An amputation may have saved her, but she chose to keep the use of both arms and perform an operation to save Heath's life.

Abandoning the home he has shared with Andrea and Carl, Rick makes a big decision – to leave behind the telephone he has been dragging around since the collapse of the prison and had used to

Negan's leadership is fascistic. He breaks social bonds and reforges them into a web in which he sits at the center.

talk to his dead wife. It's a clear sign he has finally healed the psychological wounds caused by the death of Lori and his baby daughter, Judith.

Cojones Or No Cojones

Returning to the Sanctuary, Negan sets about interrogating Eugene, promising to start cutting pieces off (in particularly delicate areas) if he doesn't cooperate. Eugene is left to reflect on this threat. Dwight sneaks in to his cell

and reveals that he is working with Rick. Eugene doesn't trust the man who killed his friend Abraham Ford, but matters are forced by the arrival of Carson, who has overheard them. Carson offers to help Eugene and the others escape if he can leave with them. Although he acknowledges the Sanctuary is safe, Carson says he has had enough of the constant fear of Negan and wants to see his brother again, Harlan Carson, who is the Hilltop's doctor.

Denise and Carson's examples point to differences between the sides of this conflict. Negan's leadership is fascistic, based around brutally enforced rules. He breaks social bonds between individuals and reforges them into a web in which he sits at

the center. His people live with this because, as Carson concedes, he provides food, shelter, and safety. But in breaking people apart, such as the Carson brothers, or Dwight and his former wife, Sherry, he also creates resentment and pain that foments rebellion.

Rick's style of leadership is democratic. People are entrusted to their own devices so long as they contribute to the overall health of the community. Relationships develop naturally. Skills are defined and roles assigned, creating a sense of community. This leads to social bonds so strong they inspire loyalty and self-sacrifice.

Nowhere's Safe

At the Hilltop, the influx of Alexandrian refugees strains food supplies. The situation is eased when Ezekiel (influenced by

Michonne) reconsiders his decision for The Kingdom to leave the war and contributes his forces and resources to the cause. Rick sets about planning defenses against the next attack. They will move the most vulnerable people out for their safety and send a small force to create a staging area nearby. This group will be in a position to outflank Negan.

Meanwhile, Negan is also planning his attack and has come up with a horrible and insidious terror tactic. If the Saviors dip their weapons in walker blood, it won't be vital to get a confirmed kill. A wound, even a scratch, will eventually result in death. Negan is always early: like The Spanish Inquisition, his chief weapon is surprise… well, surprise and walker-blood encrusted combat knives.

True to form, the Saviors attack before Rick's plans can be entirely implemented. A truck smashes through the perimeter wall and walkers flood in. As forces disperse among the tightly packed caravans inside the perimeter, the fighting is played out in confined quarters and is especially brutal. Negan cannot believe his luck when he manages to sneak up on his main enemy, Rick, from behind.

He turns to Dwight to deliver the killing blow, using his crossbow to wound Rick with one of his 'dirty' bolts. Even though the Saviors are eventually driven away, outright victory was not Negan's aim.

Dirty Tactics

Aided by Carson, Eugene and his team have escaped the Sanctuary and, after a difficult journey, arrive in time to aid in the walker clean-up. Eugene is shocked by the situation. Alexandria is abandoned. People are mysteriously falling sick. Rick is injured.

Eugene updates Rick, saying he does not feel that the Saviors have the skills to use his equipment to manufacture ammo. He considered taking his own life when caught, but didn't think the situation 'dire' enough. Now he wonders if the situation *is* perhaps that dire.

It soon becomes obvious to all that the Saviors have used 'chemical' weapons. Alexandria resident Nicholas, a man who once was trying to lead a rebellion against Rick (in Volume 15, 'We Find Ourselves'), was slashed across the back by a Savior's machete in the battle. It was a glancing blow, but he develops a fever and now lies in the infirmary as the infection slowly kills him.

His wife, Paula, and son, Mikey, are with him. Paula helps him confront and accept his mortal situation, telling him he is the reason she and Mikey have survived and will continue to survive. Carl 'comforts' Mikey, telling him that the adults will ask him to get

> Carl has seen and done things none of the other children have, and this has provided him with a very different outlook on the world.

over this. He should not, he should hold fast to his feelings, because they are "too easy to lose." As the youngest of the main characters, Carl has spent more of his life in the post-apocalyptic world than anyone. He has seen and done things none of the other children have, and this has provided him with a very different outlook on the world. Mikey seems unsure of Carl's advice. Is Carl strong, or showing signs of psychosis?

Mano A Mano

Eventually, Rick recovers. Fortunately for Rick, Dwight was still on his side, using a non-infected bolt. Knowing Negan

> Negan is always early. Like The Spanish Inquisition, his chief weapon is surprise.

IN A NUTSHELL

TITLE: 'All Out War, Part Two'
FEATURED ISSUES: #121 to 126
COLLECTION: Volume 21
SYNOPSIS: If the first part of 'All Out War' finished honors even between the opposing forces led by Rick and Negan, then part two settles the war once and for all. A lot happens in this part, including Eugene's capture by Negan (and escape with the help of some discontent Saviors); Rick abandoning the partially destroyed Alexandria to set up a new base in Hilltop; Negan's deadly assault on Hilltop; Rick's recovery from Dwight's untainted crossbow bolt to the surprise of Negan; and Rick and Negan coming to an understanding about the futility of war, just before Rick slits his throat, finally bringing the conflict to a resolution. Lucky for Negan, Rick is in an unforgiving mood and he ensures Negan survives his injury so that he can rot in a jail and pay for his crimes.

TIDBITS:

- We learn that Jesus is gay with the introduction of his boyfriend Alex.

- Carson and several other Saviors defect from Negan's rule with Eugene to join Rick's army, proving that although feared Negan is perhaps not the most inspirational of leaders.

- Carl's 'consoling' advice to Mikey after the death of his father, Nicholas, is both chilling and a sign of where Carl is mentally. He warns Mikey to ignore the advice of others on how to get over the death: "Don't listen to them. Hold onto it. Remember it... Don't let yourself forget it. It's too easy to lose."

- Artist Dave Stewart and inker Stefano Gaudiano remained onboard throughout the 'All Out War' series, to help out regular artist Charlie Adlard meet the increased publishing frequency. Stewart created the colored cover art for all 12 issues, while Gaudiano inked the interiors, leaving Adlard to illustrate the internal panels.

Rick's style of leadership is democratic. People are entrusted to their own devices so long as they contribute to the overall health of the community.

possible barter system, Rick pulls out a knife and shockingly slashes his neck. With Negan bleeding in the dirt, Rick tells the Saviors that the Hilltop's doctor can save him if they leave. The strategy is clear. Rick has made his pitch for their hearts and minds (even apparently succeeding with Negan), but knows there will be a Savior hardcore who will fight to the death for their leader. Negan *has* to be removed from the chessboard.

Negan will not go quietly though; he still has enough strength to tackle Rick. Dwight stops the other Saviors from intervening, but then Michonne and Jesus' flanking group rush them from behind. Dwight enters the fray, shooting a Savior fighting Ezekiel. He picks up Lucille, Negan's trademark baseball bat, declaring the war is over. Negan has fallen, and if the remaining Saviors

thinks him dead, Rick now sees a window of opportunity to surprise and defeat him. Drunk with triumph, Negan is yelling about urinating over Rick's corpse (much to Dwight's disgust). Overconfident, he expects a speedy surrender from Hilltop and is shocked when Rick appears on the barricades.

Now Robert Kirkman takes his biggest gamble with the story: 'All Out War' has been action-packed and the stage is ready for an explosive finale. Instead, the final conflict is an intimate and personal clash.

Negan offers to take his men back to the Sanctuary if the communities bend the knee and go back to supplying him. The last thing Negan actually wants is to wipe them out. The Saviors are not self-sufficient – they need these communities. A total victory would ultimately be a defeat.

Knowing Negan thinks him dead, Rick sees a window of opportunity.

Rick knows this is a weakness that he can exploit. He offers Negan a third way, neither surrender, nor war. Hilltop, Alexandria and The Kingdom are self-sufficient. If the battle was initially against the walkers, it is now over. They won. Everything would be good in this new society if it weren't for Negan, the playground bully who keeps messing things up because he can't figure this out. So, Rick presents an offer to the Saviors: "Make us some blankets. Bring us tools. Gather up cloth for us to make new clothes. Or just make new clothes and give them to us. Do something productive."

Negan is dumbfounded – he actually seems to have never reckoned on this. As he starts to ponder the details of a

want to survive they must retreat. "We don't have to be afraid of him or his rules anymore," he declares.

The Aftermath

Dr Carson rushes to Rick's aid, but Rick insists he save Negan. Later in the infirmary, Andrea tells Rick they should publicly execute Negan. "That's not who we are," Rick says adamantly. It has been a rough road to this point, but Rick's decision is a major step towards rebuilding civilization. Maggie asks if he really plans to let the man who killed Glenn live? Rick replies: "He lives because we are better than that. Better than him." An unsure Maggie concedes: "I think Glenn would have liked that."

If the battle was initially against the walkers, it is now over. They won. Everything would be good in this new society if it weren't for Negan.

Rick discovers Carl standing over Negan's unconscious body holding a gun. Rick may have convinced Andrea and Maggie that Negan must live, but not his son.

Rick discovers Carl standing over Negan's unconscious body holding a gun. Rick may have convinced Andrea and Maggie that Negan must live, but not his son. Rick explains Negan will be punished but "in a civilized way." Carl appears to accept this... for now.

Negan wakes and Rick explains to him his plan is to rebuild, but Negan won't be part of his vision for the future. Instead, Negan is going to rot in a cell until he dies. Rehabilitation is not a concept Rick is willing to contemplate. Is Rick taking the right course of action in letting a serpent live in his garden, albeit in a cage? This question isn't answered for many issues to come.

Overall, 'All Out War' feels like the end of a chapter in the story. Negan is defeated, the communities will rebuild, and the walker threat is subsiding into a background noise so familiar that people barely hear it anymore.

So where could Kirkman go next? We think the answer surprised everyone. •

MAKING A SPLASH

One of the highlights of Charlie Adlard's artwork is his tremendous splash panels (aka full-page or double-page illustrations). Although he uses these splash panels relatively sparingly, when he does do them they are strikingly memorable. *TWDM* looks at our choice of one of his most impactful splashes of the series. **WORDS:** Dan Auty

SO HOW DID WE GET HERE?

This splash appears in issue 150. Rick Grimes has been viciously attacked by locals, Vincent and Morton, in Alexandria, who believe that he is not taking suitable action against the Whisperers.

Rick assembles the people of the town and tells them that the time has come to fight back. He publicly forgives Vincent, and tells the crowd that the communities must now come together to stop the Whisperers.

WHAT'S THE SCENE?

Rick stands with his back to us, looking out at the Alexandria residents (some familiar, some not so much), having completed his rousing speech. They face him with their arms raised, calling his name in support for his decision. "Rick Grimes! Rick Grimes! Rick Grimes!"

MEDIUM COOL

This splash is unusual among those that Charlie Adlard has pictured over the years. It is neither a spectacular vista of approaching zombie or human enemies, nor a close-up of some dramatic character-based moment. It's a medium shot, and while it follows a fairly dramatic scene, it doesn't seem like a something that demands two pages. With the exception of a more cautious Paul Monroe, every character is doing the same thing, and it's hardly the first time Rick has delivered an inspiring speech. However, it soon becomes clear why a full two pages was used for this moment.

WHAT LIES BENEATH

This inspiring energy is immediately switched to something darker on the next page. We cut to Negan in his cell, the calls of Rick's name echoing around the room. With a dark smile, he says "Atta boy" — and we remember: Rick's decision to take charge is a direct result of a chat with his great nemesis, in which Negan advised him to tell the people what they wanted, not what he believes. Negan might be imprisoned, but his influence remains. This whole splash is built on empty promises. •

THE SECRET DIARY OF A WALKER

It's not easy being a zombie in *The Walking Dead* world, as our week in the life/death of an undead walker reveals. Diary entries transcribed by Stuart Barr.

MONDAY

Used to be this highway was gridlocked morning 'til noon. Mouthbreathers sitting in their air-conditioned tin cells listening to Bobby Bones on WMZQ. If you opened the window and tried to smell the air, you'd choke. Then all the engines stopped.

TUESDAY

It's quiet now. We wander the lanes looking for something nice to eat. The white lines lead us on. Was a time meat was plentiful — even if you couldn't catch a breather you might find a ripe possum flattened by the vehicles. One time, we found a bear that had been struck by a VW van doing about 90. What a mess that was. It was just like dining on Yogi Bear and the Scooby Gang.

WEDNESDAY

Been weeks now and haven't seen sight of any prey. There's so many of us now, and

so few of them. I'm so hungry I've tried chewing on tire rubber.

THURSDAY

Fell into a gas station dumpster. Ate some used diapers and half an old bag of candy. The diapers tasted better. Took most of the afternoon to get out, slipping around in dumpster juice. At least now I smell fabulous.

FRIDAY

A-ho! Finally, a sighting of human prey. A skinny hippy in a woolly hat. Gimme… Drat! Some other stinky has got there first… Whoa — he knows Kung Fu! Oof! He's got some mad skills this one. Still, let's have at him… Oh… I'm flying! Hey, there's another dude below! Maybe I'll get lucky and land on him. •

ALL
OUT
CHANGE

In a bold move, following the end of the epic 'All Out War' storyline in issue 126, Robert Kirkman decided to propel the story forward a few years, leaving readers not only intrigued by their new surroundings but also left wondering what happened in the missing gap. *TWDM* takes a look at the 'time jump' and discovers how it has and will affect *The Walking Dead*, with a little help from those who know.

INTERVIEWS: Dan Auty & Tara Bennett WORDS: Dan Auty

For many readers of *The Walking Dead*, issue 127 opens with one of the biggest surprises of the entire series. But this wasn't a depiction of gut-churning violence, or the shocking death of a much-loved character. Instead, we are thrown into the middle of a tense situation with a group of characters we have never seen before – Magna? Yumiko? – and we are eight pages in before encountering someone we recognize. But even then, something seems different. It's definitely Paul 'Jesus' Monroe on horseback, but wielding a sword and wearing armor, his hair pulled back like some zombie-fighting samurai. What on earth is going on?

Finally, on page 21, we see Rick – fully bearded, a hook on his arm stump. Carl is the final confirmation that something is up – he looks older, taller, clearly someone in his mid-teens who is very quickly approaching adulthood. A jump in time is the only explanation.

"I WANTED A LONG PERIOD OF PEACE, WHERE EVERYBODY HAS A PRETTY MELLOW LIFE AND EVERYBODY REBUILDS."
ROBERT KIRKMAN

THE WRITE STUFF

Robert Kirkman's decision to skip forward two years after the end of the epic 'All Out War' saga was, on the face of it, a bold one. While that storyline reached an entirely satisfying conclusion, would fans that had spent a decade reading the comic, charting the characters and the drama, feel short-changed that there were now two entire years worth of events that they would never get to see? And would readers feel like they were back at square one, with a whole load of new characters and situations introduced cold with no warning or build-up?

But as Kirkman himself explains, from a narrative perspective, the time jump was a necessary one. 'All Out War' was such a 'big' story, both in terms of length and the scale of the violence and life-changing events, that following it literally the next day might have seemed like a massive anti-climax. Respite was needed – but equally, so was a new issue a few weeks later.

Nevertheless, Kirkman was initially reluctant to go down this route. "I've stated publicly that I'm not a huge fan of time jumps and I never really wanted to do it," he says. "But after getting into 'All Out War' and working on the details of that story, I started looking at my far-reaching plans for the comic. In order for this particular story to have a pay-off and for everything that Rick has done to work, I wanted there to be something meaningful that comes from it."

"IT'S ROUGHLY TWO YEARS ON, SO YOU CAN'T GO MAD [WITH THE ART]. IN THE GRAND TRADITION OF *THE WALKING DEAD*, IT'S ALL BEEN DONE AS REALISTICALLY AS POSSIBLE."
CHARLIE ADLARD

Kirkman elaborates: "What I wanted was a long period of peace, where everybody has a pretty mellow life and everybody rebuilds. So I started getting into it, and my first thoughts were: 'Alright, here's the issue, they build a windmill. This is the issue where they move a house over here.' And I quickly realized that these were not going to be exciting comics.

"I did consider doing it without a lot of zombies, and just some action every now and then. But then I started to get really excited about moving ahead to where we are now, when things get interesting. Ultimately, I figured this was the best thing for the series."

DRAWING BLOOD

The decision to skip forward two years has had an impact on everyone involved with *The Walking Dead*, not just its creator and writer. Series artist Charlie Adlard was immediately presented with a set of unique challenges, something that Kirkman recognized early on.

"I knew it would be pretty intensive for Charlie, because he'd have to come up with the new looks for all of the characters," he admits.

In order for the jump to work, both writer and artist had to be entirely in sync with how they were going to handle the changes. "In the last few years, we have both become so busy that we have to be really conscious of talking to each other," admits Adlard, who lives and works in England, thousands of miles from Kirkman. "Just over a year ago, Robert and I sat down and said we must make the effort. And so we had our longest Skype conversation ever about when we were going to make the leap."

Adlard makes it clear that the big challenge for him wasn't so much creating the brand new characters, but how to handle the physical changes for the existing

> **"I STARTED TO GET REALLY EXCITED ABOUT MOVING AHEAD TO WHERE WE ARE NOW, WHEN THINGS GET INTERESTING. I FIGURED THIS WAS THE BEST THING FOR THE SERIES."** ROBERT KIRKMAN

protagonists. "It's roughly two years on, so you can't go mad," he explains. "Certain characters, like Carl, will physically grow from a 13-year-old to a 15-year-old kid. That is a radical difference. The other characters won't look that different, so you either change them with hair, like Rick, or essentially keep them the same. In the grand tradition of *The Walking Dead*, it's all been done as realistically as possible."

While some of the 'supporting' cast remain more-or-less unchanged, Adlard did pay specific attention to his leads, ensuring that the passage of time could be clearly represented by the change in their appearances.

"I thought it would be really cool to see Rick with a beard and really shaven hair, and when Robert and I talked he came up with the same idea," Adlard says. "I have to admit aesthetically, I was really annoyed with the way Rick's hair was looking. I almost wish I could have drawn him like Andrew Lincoln, but that's not how our Rick looks.

"We had to thrash out the look of Carl between us. Robert didn't want to put him in some ridiculous iron mask, so that was a little bit of a struggle. Negan was fairly obvious – he couldn't be clean-shaven anymore."

"AESTHETICALLY, I WAS REALLY ANNOYED WITH RICK'S HAIR. I WISH I COULD HAVE DRAWN HIM LIKE ANDREW LINCOLN, BUT THAT'S NOT HOW OUR RICK LOOKS."
CHARLIE ADLARD

THINGS CHANGE

The human characters are only part of the story. The other vital element that would also be affected by the passing of time was the zombies themselves. Adlard has in the past spoken about how his depiction of the living dead over the last decade is designed to show a gradual but definite increase in their level of decay. Would a sudden jump of two years affect either their physical appearance or behavior?

For Kirkman, it's more or less business as usual, but he does shed some interesting light on how the undead 'survive.' "Whatever turned them into zombies is preserving them to a certain extent," he reveals. "We've also established that winter keeps them preserved, and we've lived through a few of those. Also, it's not like every zombie we encounter has existed since day one of the apocalypse. There aren't a lot of people, so I wouldn't say zombies are being made every day, but there are new zombies being thrown into the mix. It's going to be a problem for a long time."

Adlard agrees: "There are always one or two fresher zombies, because people are still getting bitten. But I am increasingly conscious when drawing a more 'generic' zombie, because the majority are disintegrating. Personally that is an issue for me, to get them looking more monstrous."

"THERE ARE ALWAYS ONE OR TWO FRESHER ZOMBIES, BECAUSE PEOPLE ARE STILL GETTING BITTEN... BUT THE MAJORITY ARE DISINTEGRATING."
CHARLIE ADLARD

"WHATEVER TURNED THEM INTO ZOMBIES IS PRESERVING THEM TO A CERTAIN EXTENT. THEY'RE GOING TO BE A PROBLEM FOR A LONG TIME." ROBERT KIRKMAN

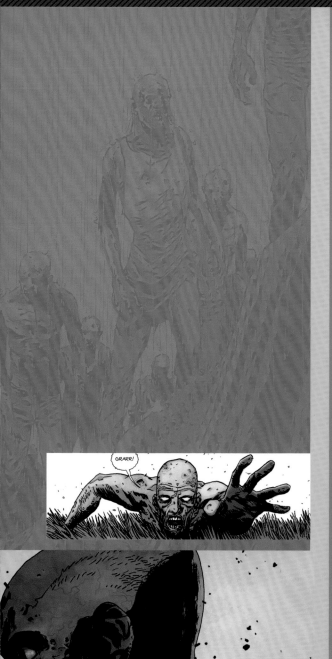

WRAP STARS

Once the decision to make the time jump was made, it was met with an enthusiastic response elsewhere at Kirkman's company, Skybound Entertainment. But just as Kirkman and Adlard had considerable narrative and artistic logistics to work out, there were various practical and commercial issues that also needed to be addressed.

Shawn Kirkham, Skybound's business development director, reveals that the plans were as much a surprise to him as to anyone. "I knew something big was going to happen after 'All Out War,' but didn't really know what was in store. When Robert broke it to us, we were as floored as the readers were," he laughs. "It was just a few months in advance, and there really wasn't much warning for any of us. Even though we all work closely in the office, Robert still likes to keep the story aspects of *The Walking Dead* as much of a secret as he can."

> "CHANGES THIS BIG ARE RARELY KEPT UNDER WRAPS, BUT THIS WAS A FAR MORE ORGANIC, STORY-DRIVEN CHANGE. OUR PLAN WAS TO KEEP IT SECRET THE WHOLE TIME."
> **SEAN MACKIEWICZ**

For editorial director Sean Mackiewicz, one of the biggest challenges was keeping this radical development a secret from both fans and press. As he explains: "Changes this big are rarely kept under wraps, as publishers want to push more books out the door. DC and Marvel can't go a month without spoiling a death or identity change, but this was a far more organic, story-driven change. Our plan was to keep it a secret the whole time.

"The only indication that something was up was releasing a double-sized issue for $2.99, right after the most high profile storyline in the history of the book. Charlie drew up promos, to show how much the main cast has changed over the course of the series, but we didn't release those until after the issue hit."

> ## "THE REAL CHALLENGE WAS FIGURING OUT FUN WAYS TO PRESENT THE CHANGE OUTSIDE THE COMIC, WHETHER LOUDLY OR REFLECTING IT IN MERCHANDISE."
> SEAN MACKIEWICZ

FRESH FLESH

Both Kirkham and Mackiewicz recognize that the dramatic change in some characters – plus the introduction of brand new ones – would affect the way the property was represented beyond the pages of the comic, both

in terms of publicity and licensing deals with other companies.

"The real challenge was figuring out fun ways to present these changes outside the comic, whether loudly, like the banner art at the top of our booth at San Diego Comic-Con in July, or reflecting them in our toys and other merchandise," says Mackiewicz.

"We definitely had to reassess some things," admits Kirkham. "But thankfully *The Walking Dead* universe is pretty vast. We've got more than 10 years of stories to play around with, and that leaves a lot of room for our business partners.

"At the end of the day, we're excited to see what we can come up with for merchandise, based on the new looks of our favorite characters. I can't wait to see some of these characters out there in the wild."

For all the logistical issues the time jump might have caused both creatively and from a business angle, everyone agrees that it has presented any number of exciting possibilities for the future. Kirkman is being careful to slowly reveal the fate of many of his cast – most notably Michonne – and Adlard is enthusiastic about his role in crafting some new environments.

"Visually it's exciting, because we've never really seen the interior of The Kingdom," he says. "It's always been the buses and the campsite and the auditorium of the school. We've not really seen much of the community living within, so that will be interesting to draw. We'll have to wait and see who is alive in there!"

Kirkman puts it even more plainly, revealing how important the time jump was to both his and Adlard's enthusiasm in putting together such a regular, long-running comic book: "It re-energized him, and the same for me too. We're really excited about what is coming next." •

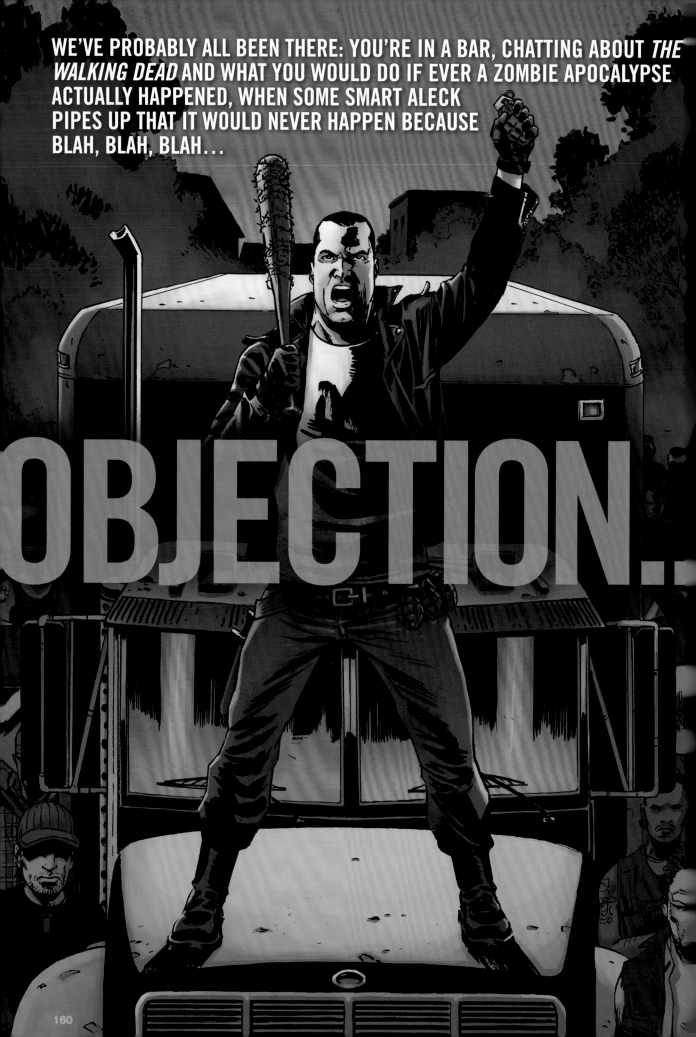

WE'VE PROBABLY ALL BEEN THERE: YOU'RE IN A BAR, CHATTING ABOUT *THE WALKING DEAD* AND WHAT YOU WOULD DO IF EVER A ZOMBIE APOCALYPSE ACTUALLY HAPPENED, WHEN SOME SMART ALECK PIPES UP THAT IT WOULD NEVER HAPPEN BECAUSE BLAH, BLAH, BLAH...

OBJECTION...

OVERRULED

...WELL, *TWDM* HAS HEARD ALL THEIR OBJECTIONS, AND HERE'S WHAT WE HAVE TO SAY IN RESPONSE: "OVERRULED!"
WORDS: DAN AUTY

Everyone loves zombies... unless you are *actually* a survivor of an undead apocalypse. But if you're reading this then we're going to take the chance that you aren't and you love zombies as much as we do. Zombies have long been a favorite villain in horror films, books, comics and on TV, and their popularity is now at an all-time high. Vampires might have the charm, ghosts the spooky wailing, and werewolves the, er, hair, but when it comes to tapping into our most primal fears and providing the opportunity for some thrilling gore-splattered horror action, then zombies are clearly the monster of choice.

But are they actually that much of a threat? There's no doubt that *The Walking Dead* has showcased some brilliant stories and characters, both on the page and off it, but much of this is down to the human drama, not because of the actual walkers. Are Rick and friends just making a lot of fuss over nothing? Are they, in fact, just not very good at surviving in a world populated by a rather ineffectual monster? We present the case...

OBJECTION: You can dodge round them and run away

Let's face it, zombies aren't fast. In fact, you will struggle to find a slower adversary than a shambling walker. (A biter, perhaps? They are too lazy even to shamble and just wait for their victims to stumble their way.) Half the time, a walker's legs are on the verge of dropping off through decay, and even fresher zombies move with that unique walk that lies halfway between a limp and a lurch. These aren't The Running Dead after all, and even if they present more of a threat in larger numbers, they are still just shambling at roughly the same speed. They can't drive, they can't swim and you should see them trying to go up stairs. Run away – they won't catch you!

OBJECTION OVERRULED!
Yes, zombies are slow. And yes, it is easy to run away from them. But are you going to run forever? As time goes on, there are going to be more and more walkers around; run in one direction and you are likely to find another bunch of flesh-eaters staggering towards you. Turn around, and there are yet more hungry mouths chomping. Even an Olympic marathon runner is going to tire eventually. The walkers are not. At some point, you will have to stop to drink, eat, rest and recuperate. The walkers won't. They are the very definition of the unstoppable force...

SHIT!

OBJECTION: OK, so we'd just find a safe place to stop and rest

You've been running non-stop for four hours, say, dodging around walkers. You have managed to get away and you think you have spotted somewhere that looks secure. You pop inside, cook up some food, go to the toilet (hey – there's no escaping biology!), have a nap, and relax, safe in the knowledge that no walker can get in. Fully rested the next day, you're ready to get going again.

OBJECTION OVERRULED!
Firstly, how many of us can run for four hours non-stop? And then be ready to do it again the next day? And the next? And the next? Yeah, right!

Secondly, you open the door to find your safe haven has been swarmed by hundreds of zombies. They know you are in there, and there's no way you can fight through them and escape. The only option is to retreat back into your bunker. All of a sudden, your safe haven has become a deathtrap. And we hope you enjoy drinking urine, because your water bottle is almost empty!

Humans need food and especially clean water to survive, so inevitably we will end up congregating near handy supplies of these. It's not going to take long before the zombies figure that out and start congregating too.

OBJECTION: Zombies are stupid

It's not hard to work out a walker's game plan. It is going to walk in a semi-straight line towards you, and when it reaches you, it is going to eat you. It is not about to secretly plot some cunning double bluff, or befriend you before devouring you, or distract you with a dance routine while its buddy sneaks up on you from behind. If you can't outwit a zombie then you probably deserve to get chomped a little.

OBJECTION OVERRULED!
Having no plan at all is way better than having a plan that goes horribly wrong. It's easy to get complacent when you think you know exactly what your enemy is going to do, even one as predictable as a walker. That's the moment they suddenly appear from behind a tree and start chowing down.

OBJECTION: They are weak too

The undead aren't known for their time spent in the gym, and the amount of human flesh they eat has no effect on their bulk or health. They are falling apart, barely held together by rotting flesh and crumbling bones. They are not going to put up much of a fight when they finally reach you. Admittedly, you do need to watch out for their twitching jaws, but as long as you can knock them on the ground, it shouldn't be too hard to make mush of their craniums.

OBJECTION OVERRULED!
Zombies only want to do one thing – eat you. Unlike the living, they aren't going to retreat when you start fighting back, and they will stop at nothing to get their teeth into you. And in a group? Forget it! While you are trying to knock one walker to the ground, there's another one already down there, about to chomp on your ankles.

OK, so they might be individually weak, but because they feel no pain,

and the fact that you have to destroy their brains through pretty thick bone (we hope you've never tried bashing someone's skull in, but we imagine it's a lot harder to penetrate than just a quick jab with a fork), makes them a tricky enemy to dispatch over and over again. A hundred enemies is a minimum of a hundred swings of an axe – gotta be super fit to survive!

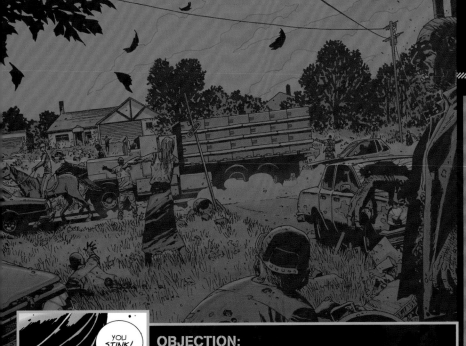

OBJECTION: The military would soon sort them out

The US armed forces is pretty big. There are around 1.1 million personnel currently serving in the armed forces in the US alone, not including those serving abroad and the reserves. They also have access to some rather fearsome weaponry, everything from the modern M16 assault rifle to the very devastating Javelin missile. A zombie has, well, its teeth. As soon as a zombie infection is detected, the army would move in, contain the area and dispatch the infected quickly and clinically.

OBJECTION OVERRULED!

Firstly, a zombie virus spreads fast. Forget Ebola, this thing is super virulent, turning the living into the dead in a matter of minutes; seconds in some cases. By the time the military mobilizes to mount a response, the zombie army could already be into the hundreds of thousands, whole cities could have fallen.

Also, zombies only die from headshots, otherwise they keep coming, so accuracy would be a factor – firing a whole magazine into them won't do much good unless the head is hit. Soldiers are trained to shoot, but that's still a high level of sustained accuracy. And talk about battle fatigue – the horror of warfare is just that when your enemy is a swathe of flesh-hungry undead monsters.

Finally, where there are zombies, there are living humans too. Collateral damage is a common term used in warfare, but this is less easy to accept when it's your fellow countrymen taking the hit.

OBJECTION: Zombies' noses are easily fooled

When it comes to seeking their prey, walkers rely primarily on their ears and noses. Which means that covering yourself in foul zombie goo and strolling in their midst is an easy way to avoid being attacked. You could walk for miles alongside them without being spotted, just as long as you're nice and stinky and maybe let out the occasional ghoulish groan, just to be respectful. Rick and Glenn did it, Michonne did it, Carol did it. Easy! So slap on that putrid gloop and chill out.

OBJECTION OVERRULED!

If you're attempting a daring escape from a tight spot, then the all-over body-gunk routine works wonders. But all the time? You wanna walk around smelling like that? The human race has been decimated and the opportunities for meeting new allies, friends or lovers aren't exactly plentiful, so permanently stinking like a five-month-old corpse left out in the Georgian sun isn't exactly going to endear you to potential new pals or partners.

OBJECTION: Just stay quiet

Let's face it, a high majority of zombie attacks in *The Walking Dead* are a direct result of humans being idiotically loud. Whether it's firing guns unnecessarily, shouting, screaming or crashing through woodland, our heroes have a hard time keeping the noise down. And if there's one thing that is sure to attract the attention of the living dead, it's noisy humans. You want to avoid being eaten? Shut the hell up!

OBJECTION OVERRULED!

Sensible in theory, but utterly redundant in practice. True, noise does attract zombies, but most of this noise is created while already under attack. Why are we firing a gun? Because a walker is attacking us and we don't have a machete or a crossbow. Why are we screaming at the top of our lungs? Because a walker is eating our legs...

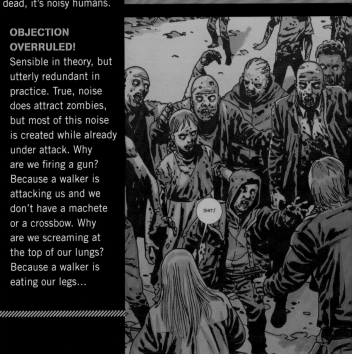

OBJECTION: So just take off and nuke them from orbit

It's the only way to be sure, right? A nuclear weapon would certainly decimate a zombie horde. A high yield bomb would incinerate zombies as much as any living thing within the blast area. Outside of the immediate area, who knows what effect the resulting radiation would have on the living dead, but it wouldn't be pretty.

OBJECTION OVERRULED!

This option would work if the outbreak is localized in one city, say, but what if it's as widespread as it is in *The Walking Dead*? What are we gonna do, nuke America? We see the future, and it is Charlton Heston kneeling on a beach in his pants shouting, "Goddamn you all to hell!" Simply not an option, even as a last resort.

Of course, China, North Korea, Russia, the UK or any other nuclear power might think differently if they wanted to stop the infection from spreading outside of North America.

OBJECTION OVERRULED!

Wit, charm, secrets, mystery... who cares? These things aren't scary. They aren't going to make you run screaming for your life or deliver gallons of guts and gore. Zombies cut through the nonsense and get straight to the point. They are everywhere and they want to kill you. What more could anyone want from a terrifying post-apocalyptic nightmare? •

OBJECTION: Zombies are boring

What makes zombies an effective adversary – mindless, shambling undead hordes staggering ever onwards towards a common prey – also makes them about the dullest antagonist you could think of. They all look the same, they all smell the same, they all do the same thing. You can't engage them in stimulating debate as to the nature of evil or attempt to uncover the mystery of what they want. It might look like Rick and his group have their hands full, but I bet any of them would jump at the chance to confront a cultured psychopath, tentacled demon or vengeful poltergeist, just to break up the monotony of the boring dead.

Fans of the TV show are just getting to know who Negan and his Saviors are, but for readers of the comic, a lot has happened since then. After Negan is ultimately defeated and a period of relative peace occurs, a new threat arises: the Whisperers. At the time of writing, an intense and brutal war between Rick's forces and the might of the Whisperers was in full swing. So here's a rundown of the events that led up to this monumental new story arc, which has comic book readers gripped.

WORDS: Stuart Barr

The road to 'The Whisperer War' begins in the aftermath of 'All Out War,' the epic 12-parter that ran in issues 115-126. So, here's a quick refresher of events that happened in-between: after the fall of Negan, a two-year time-skip follows. Alexandria, Hilltop, The Kingdom, and even the Sanctuary have grown ties of support, trade and dependency under the respective leaders of Rick (who is also the overall 'president' of the new society), Maggie, Ezekiel, and Dwight. The walkers have very much become a background threat, ever-present but, like tinnitus, manageable. But then a new horror emerges to threaten this peace: walkers that can talk and use weapons.

Naturally, they aren't really undead but humans pretending to be walkers. Called the Whisperers, they are unlike any antagonists we have come across in *The Walking Dead* before. They hide in plain sight, wearing harvested skins, like Leatherface in *The Texas Chain Saw Massacre*. It is a development of a technique we saw Rick Grimes use when Alexandria was overrun by walkers in issue

83, only far more extreme. By wearing the flayed skins of corpses, the Whisperers walk among the undead completely without fear.

Organized like a cult, their leader is a woman called Alpha. She also has a second-in-command/enforcer, known as Beta, and a daughter, Lydia. A brutal hierarchy exists within this new group. Strength is prized and weakness is punished. They view themselves as animals and no longer human. They also don't like other humans threatening their borders and aren't afraid to kill.

As Alexandria and neighboring settlements have grown, more and more people travel between each community, and inevitably some have strayed into the Whisperers realm. Alpha does not like this at all and exercises some pretty visceral tactics to mark the Whisperers borders, namely sticking the heads of several recognizable characters (including Rosita and Ezekiel) on spikes. Naturally, this scares the hell out of Rick's now very large community, who start to question his rule.

BY WEARING THE FLAYED SKINS OF CORPSES, THE WHISPERERS WALK AMONG THE UNDEAD COMPLETELY WITHOUT FEAR.

TOO MANY PROBLEMS

One of Rick's biggest problems is that, before the war with the Saviors, there were no strangers in their relatively small communities and residents knew every face. It is now possible for an unmasked Whisperer assassin (they look predictably normal without their skin suits) to slip into Alexandria and kill whoever they like.

Even more problematic is that in the two years of peace that followed Negan's downfall, Rick has set up a rule of law, but without a direct threat, there was no real need for a military force. The Whisperers seriously expose this flaw, and a militia is hastily established to combat the threat. When Dwight resigns from leading the Saviors, he walks straight into a new role leading and training the militia. His military training makes him uniquely capable. However, Dwight's

I AM ALPHA... AND I SHOW YOU MY FACE BECAUSE WE MEAN YOU NO HARM.

WE ONLY WANT ONE THING FROM YOU...

...MY DAUGHTER.

IT'S SURPRISING THAT RICK DOESN'T SEEM AWARE OF HOW MUCH NEGAN IS MANIPULATING HIM AGAIN.

> WOULD I BE CORRECT IN ASSUMING YOU'RE LOOKING FOR A GROUP WHO CAN HELP YOU GET REVENGE ON THE PEOPLE WHO EXILED YOU?

abdication of leadership creates a power vacuum at the Sanctuary and they are not willing to join the fight against the Whisperers.

Although a new Savior leader has yet to emerge, there is an older one close at hand. At the end of 'All Out War,' Negan was imprisoned rather than executed. When challenged on this decision, Rick's mantra was always "we don't do that now." But keeping Negan in a cell is like opening a play with a handgun on a table: at some point, you know it is going to go off. Inevitably, after years of biding his time, Negan escapes and heads straight to the Whisperers.

What happens then is surprising. Negan's willingness to join this 'cult of the anti-self' is at odds with his character. Alpha, and especially Beta, are suspicious of his motives. We already know Negan is a master manipulator and he easily gets Alpha on his side. Naturally, it's a ploy – this is Negan after all. Once he's close enough to Alpha, he simply kills her, returning to Rick with her severed head. It's a uniquely Negan take on a 'gesture of goodwill.' It's also the incident that instigates 'The Whisperer War.'

> SVAASH!

> IT'S REALLY HER...

> THIS ISN'T GOING TO BE A LAND WAR.

> WE'RE NOT FIGHTING FOR TERRITORY. THERE WON'T BE AN EFFORT TO HOLD POSITIONS, BOXING THE ENEMY OUT.

> THIS WILL BE DIFFERENT.

FORCE MAJOR

So, how is this conflict different from the one in 'All Out War'? Firstly, when Rick is discussing strategy with Dwight, he says this won't be a "land war" – a traditional conflict based on numerical supremacy involving opposing armies. The two sides facing each other in 'All Out War' were closely matched, not only in numbers but also tactics and weapons. This time, Rick is confident that they have superior firepower and strategy, and he knows that the Whisperers don't even use guns (too human!). Anyone with a popular history book on 20th century warfare

168

IN NEGAN WE TRUST?

Another significant difference is Rick's ultimate aim. Against Negan, it was to defeat the Saviors and neutralize their leader. Free of their demagogue, his people could be brought into line and made productive. The aim in the Whisperer War is extermination.

Rick has spent too many hours before the war in the company of Negan. His "we don't do that now" mantra is relatively easily discarded. It was Negan who told Rick to exploit the paranoia and fear of his people toward an external threat to deflect attention away from more pressing internal issues, such as challenges to Rick's suitability as leader. It's surprising that Rick doesn't seem

will be hearing alarm bells right about now. Rick's approach sounds not unlike the strategy that took America into Vietnam.

Even without their leader, the Whisperers are a formidable force. They can hide in plain sight, among both humans and walkers. They have a different belief system, which means they can't be reasoned with or talked down. They can essentially control the walkers, by influencing a herd's movements, and their numbers grow every time a living human dies. And their new leader, Beta, is savage and consumed with a desire to avenge Alpha.

Facing Dwight's well-armed and drilled fighters, the Whisperers expand their numbers by driving a group of walkers toward them. Overwhelmed, only Dwight's ability to develop strategy in combat saves them. Both sides take losses, but neither Rick or his forces expected any.

aware of how much Negan is manipulating him again.

However, perhaps the most important function of the Whisperer War is to make the walkers a threat again. Facing a group of roamers is a grave situation now, even for a well-armed group. The Whisperers weaponize the undead in a way no-one has done before.

THE WHISPERER WAR MAKES THE WALKERS A THREAT AGAIN... THE WHISPERERS WEAPONIZE THE UNDEAD IN A WAY NO-ONE HAS DONE BEFORE.

They even have a weapon of mass destruction, having corralled and trapped a vast herd in their territory for mobilization as an undead army.

Everything Rick and the people of the Washington area communities have built over the past two years could be destroyed, and by giving his ear to the Mephistophelian Negan, Rick is in danger of losing his soul. •

ALPHA & BETA

The Whisperers have become one of Rick's toughest challenges to overcome yet. They are a ruthless group whose way of life goes completely against his beliefs. While Rick's group believes in holding onto the remnants of humanity, Alpha's group has discarded this, believing that embracing basic animal instinct is the only way to survive. With a group as radicalized as this, its leaders, first Alpha and then Beta, believe that human empathy is a hindrance to survival more passionately than anyone else. *TWDM* learns more about these two enigmatic figures.

WORDS: Tolly Maggs

LEADER OF THE PACK

The initial encounter with the Whisperers was a small affair, with Hilltop lookouts Marco and Ken first meeting just a few of them in a small skirmish out in the wilds (issue 130). However, when the true scale of the Whisperer threat was discovered by Rick in issue 142, it became clear that this new enemy was going to incite the kind of battle he and the rest of his community had never faced before.

At the heart of all of this is their savagely efficient leader, Alpha, who we first meet in issue 132. Seemingly cold and ruthless, she (along with the rest of the Whisperers) has donned the skin of the undead, believing that the only way humanity can overcome this savage world is by shedding any empathy they have left and becoming like animals, running on instinct.

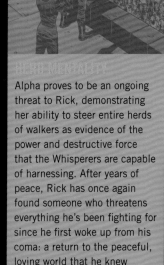

HERO MENTALITY

Alpha proves to be an ongoing threat to Rick, demonstrating her ability to steer entire herds of walkers as evidence of the power and destructive force that the Whisperers are capable of harnessing. After years of peace, Rick has once again found someone who threatens everything he's been fighting for since he first woke up from his coma: a return to the peaceful, loving world that he knew before the fall.

Alpha, however, doesn't see humanity's second chance at life this way, instead believing that they have to embrace this new world overrun with the undead, adapting to fit into

the new natural order. In her mind, empathy is a sign of human weakness that, if found in survivors, will lead to their ultimate destruction. But, despite claiming she's dismissed all emotional ties to other humans, there is one natural connection that she will never be able to truly abandon – her daughter, Lydia.

BUTTING HEADS

In a world ravished by decaying corpses that consume human flesh, acting on basic survival instincts is necessary in order to avoid death. But how long can you truly survive in a world like this? Both Rick Grimes and Alpha have endured the tests brought on by the zombie apocalypse. By proving themselves to be worthy leaders, who have both succeeded in their own unique way, their biggest competition

has become each other: in true *Walking Dead* style, the living are once again revealed as the greatest threat to survival.

As well as ensuring the protection of their individual groups, these two will also stop at nothing to protect their positions at the top. Societies need strong leaders to take charge and control any hardships they come across. While Rick is confident enough in his own abilities to

SIGNS OF WEAKNESS

Alpha's greatest weakness is her one last vestige of humanity: being a mother. She puts on a convincing performance as the leader of the Whisperers, ruthlessly cutting away anything or anyone who stands in their way. She even turns a blind eye to rape among the Whisperers by justifying the act as being natural in the animal world, stating, "only the strong survive." Her own daughter willingly abandons her and the rest of the Whisperers to go with Rick, and yet Alpha shows zero emotion, allowing her daughter to do as she pleases.

But... when she finds a moment to be alone, Alpha shows she is unable to completely let go of her connection with her daughter. She is found crying in the forest by a fellow Whisperer, who stumbles upon her at the most opportune (or perhaps that

should be inopportune) time (issue 148). Despite claiming he won't tell the others, Alpha kills the intruder anyway. While she is a naturally caring mother, she ultimately is the leader of the Whisperers and will do whatever it takes to protect that. This is the life she's chosen and come what may, she must stick to it.

establish himself as the sole leader, Alpha needs her second-in-command, Beta, to keep order among her ranks. Curiously, Beta

shows great loyalty to Alpha, when you would initially perhaps suspect he would have more of a Negan-Dwight relationship with her.

THE DEAD WILL FOLLOW YOUR SCREAMS SOON ENOUGH.

HUKK!

DOUBLE STANDARDS

Despite being adamant that the Whisperers' way is the right way to survive, Alpha also believes that her daughter will be safer in Rick's care. This admittance establishes an inner conflict that she refuses to share with anyone, at the risk of losing her position as leader of the group.

Both being parents, Rick and Alpha have more in common than they think: they both put the safety of their children above all other considerations. While Rick is open about this, Alpha hides it behind the face of a cold, efficient leader (and a mask!).

There is a moment of mutual appreciation as they realize how much they care for their children in issue 144, but this is shattered after Alpha openly admits that she allowed her daughter to be raped by others in the Whisperer group. She believes this is the ultimate way to create a unified group that can survive any challenge: discarding what's left of their humanity, along with the rules of the old world.

LYDIA ISN'T *SAFE* HERE. AT NIGHT... SOMETIMES THE MEN DO THINGS TO HER... AND HER MOTHER *LETS* THEM.

I LET THEM... HAVE MY DAUGHTER... I THOUGHT IT WOULD... MAKE HER STRONGER...

I... THOUGHT THERE WAS NO OTHER WAY TO LIVE IN THIS WORLD...

I... I MISS HER SO MUCH.

BRAWN OF THE DEAD

If Alpha is the brains of the group, Beta is the brawn. Tall and strong, Beta is an imposing force to be reckoned with, which is likely why he was chosen as Alpha's second-in-command. Quick to anger and dangerously violent, Beta demands respect from the group in his own way. Ultimately though, he has chosen to be second to Alpha. It becomes clear why in issue 156: Beta respects Alpha and it is this that helped her secure her position at the top. As Negan points out to her, the only reason why she's able to stay in control is because Beta will do anything to protect her.

STAY DOWN.

FUCK.

YOU.

NEGAN BEGINS TO REALIZE HE'S STUMBLED UPON A GROUP EVEN MORE RUTHLESS AND DEVOID OF EMPATHY THAN HIM.

THE LOADED GUN

If there's one guarantee in *The Walking Dead* it's that the presence of Negan means trouble. That's exactly what happens when he escapes his Alexandria prison and flees Rick's clutches to sign up with the Whisperers. If alarm bells weren't ringing when he and Alpha first meet (issue 143) then they soon would be.

Negan first proved his worth to Alpha by establishing his ruthless approach to survival and convincing her how similar his way is to theirs. Alpha initially seems taken in by Negan – he does have the gift of the gab, after all – and so unsurprisingly, a jealous Beta takes an immediate dislike to him. Beta's warnings fall on deaf

ears, perhaps drowned out by Negan's own inflated ego, as Alpha accepts Negan into the Whisperers, perhaps keen to share the burden of leadership with someone who has been in that position before. However, after his attempts to prevent the rape of a Whisperer are stopped by Beta (issue 156), Negan begins to realize that, unbelievably, he's stumbled upon a group of survivors even more ruthless and devoid of empathy than him.

AND THE GUN GOES BANG!

Negan's desire to join the Whisperers might have been initially genuine, but from the moment he was stopped from preventing a rape (as issue 117 revealed, Negan has very strong feelings about sexual assault) the writing was on the wall. Negan being Negan, he takes matters into his own hands and, at the first opportunity, slits Alpha's throat (issue 156).

While he sees this brash action as merely a way of ending the growing tensions between Rick's community and the Whisperers, and thus worming his way into Rick's good books, Negan has unwittingly done a lot more than just destroying the brains behind a terrifyingly dangerous group – he's left a power vacuum that gets dominated by the brawn: Beta. Without Alpha to hold him back from considering the best tactical options, Beta and the rest of the Whisperers set out to pursue blind vengeance.

VENGEANCE, THY NAME IS BETA

Alpha's leadership was based on communication, adaptation and forward-planning; on several occasions, she was seen to be well-prepared for forthcoming events and willing to adapt depending on various outcomes. Beta, on the other hand, is more like a bull in a china shop: rash, brash and unstoppably violent. He acts on gut instinct and lacks the social skills of Alpha.

Filled with rage, Beta takes charge of the group, bestowing the role of alpha upon himself. Without the original Alpha there to hold him back, Beta lets his animal instincts rule.

He becomes the *de facto* leader, which is perhaps the real shock in the comic's most recent storyline, not Alpha's death: through

him, we learn that it was only Alpha's last shred of humanity – her love for her daughter – that was stopping the Whisperers from fully embracing their feral, anarchic, animalistic nature. Their new raw unpredictability under Beta has made the Whisperers one of the series' most dangerous threats. •